THE
NOTORIOUS
POACHER

Other Books Available

The Pheasants of The World
Dr. Jean Delacour

Pheasants and Their Enemies
Dr. J. O'C. Fitzsimons

Gamekeeping and Shooting for Amateurs
Guy N. Smith

Ferreting and Trapping
Guy N. Smith

Ratting and Rabbiting
Guy N. Smith

Way of the Gamekeeper
Jill Mason

Advanced Taxidermy
P.A. O'Connor

Shotgun Shooting
John Brindle

Tom Firr of the Quorn
Roy Heron

Cockfighting and Game Fowl
Herbert Atkinson

THE NOTORIOUS POACHER

MEMOIRS OF AN OLD POACHER

By

G. BEDSON
("GRANDAD")

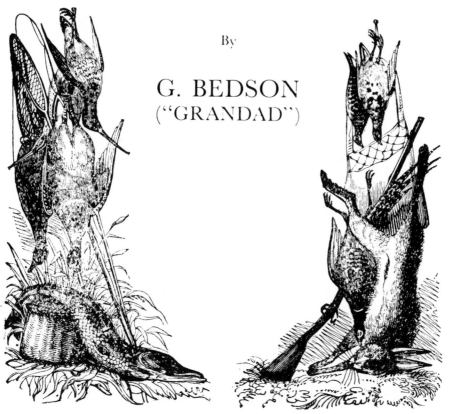

Distributor:
NIMROD BOOK SERVICES
PO Box 1
Liss, Hants, GU33 7PR
England

© Learnex (Publishers) Ltd 1985

ISBN 0 947647-42-2

First Edition 1981
Second Edition 1985
Second Impression 1986

Printed and bound by
R. J. Acford, Chichester, Sussex

Publisher:
NIMROD PRESS LTD
P.O. Box 1
LISS
Hants, GU33 7PR
England

CONTENTS

LIST OF ILLUSTRATIONS

AUTHOR'S PREFACE

This book about poaching life and the work and knowledge it takes is written mainly for my grandsons. It tells of the hard poverty in this so-called Great Britain in the early years of this century, in the early twenties and thirties when poverty was widespread throughout the country.

I carried on the poaching game from schoolboy days throughout life until disease was deliberately spread over the whole country. What you read in this book is truth and not the rubbish written by some authors. I will explain some of this rubbish as I go along.

It is a story of life which has passed on and will not return.

The big estates owned by the wealthy are dying away fast due to taxation. In spite of all arguments, when these estates were in private ownership and keepered properly, they were places of real beauty. Take the keepers off and allow public access and in a few years they are ruined.

The poaching of game in all its different ways is often a subject of conversation among people of all kinds, from gypsies to land owners and estate owners. There are a good many people who say they know this or that about the poaching of game, but in my lifetime, I have met only a few real experts at the fine arts of the game. There are authors of books and newspaper writers who have written about these subjects but, in my opinion, the majority of them have never even seen or experienced a good night's poaching. The word poacher is used to cover a lot of various actions of people, from the man shooting from a car to a boy fishing a private pond. There is a great difference between these and a man who uses nets at night-time. In the following pages is a true account of a lifetime of both day and night poaching.

"Grandad"

INTRODUCTION

As a *character* of the countryside the poacher of old was either despised as a man of no principles (a nocturnal predator) *or* as a person who was secretly admired for his skill and courage. Nobody doubted he was a rascal, but whether he was looked upon as a scoundrel or a Robin Hood depended upon the view taken.

Women, as well as men, have taken up the poaching life. It is stated that one *Granny Bab* (Mrs. Barbara Snellgrove) of Barnstaple, Devon continued to poach with great skill up to the age of ninety-four. She died in 1795 at the age of ninety-six years.

The poacher of old pitted his skill against the authority of gamekeepers and officers of the law, thus avoiding conviction. He tackled the capture of pheasants, partridges, rabbits, hares and other spoils of the countryside with nets, ferrets, dog and the occasional use of the gun. On occasions he also caught fish with hook and line, nets or spears. His knowledge of the ways of his bounty and matters relating to the countryside were legend. He was known by the gamekeeper but rarely apprehended; such was the hazardous life he led.

Poaching is an illegal occupation and, therefore, cannot be justified under any circumstances. The fact remains that poaching in the past may have been taken up from need and poverty; when the rabbit or hare may have been taken to feed hungry children. Whatever the reason, provided it is understood that the poaching described relates to *olden times*, the contents of this book may be regarded as historical.

The basis of this book is a true story, supplemented where appropriate, by references and illustrations from old books and journals. The author is still alive, but too old to practise his poaching. This is a story from the past, authentic in its descriptions of poaching and social background.

THE POEM

A poem which describes the role of the poacher appeared in an old book *Annals of Sporting*:

Extract from "*The Poacher*"

Oft to the warren, on the moor,
  When bright o'er all the moon-beam shin'd,
His ferrets and his nets he bore,
  Whilst his dark lurcher lurked behind,
And 'neath the shadow of the wall,
  One moment would he pause to see,
    In circling round the rabbits play,
    Light frisking in the silver ray
  In rapid movements light and free;
Then gave the signal—at the call
At each wide spring and rapid bound
A bleeding victim stain'd the ground,
Till deep in earth the fearful race
  Seek shelter from their sullen foe
In vain, for now the ferrets trace
  Each mazy burrow far below,
And urge them forth in wild affright;
  While Hubert stands, with ready net,
  Carefully o'er each entrance set,
To intercept them in their flight.

Far in some marshy woodland glade,
  Where slow the sluggish waters ooze
Across the track by woodcocks made,
His well-limed twigs he often laid;
  Or spread around the running nooze;
On to some fenny mere he'd go,
Where waving reeds and rushes grow,
  Where teal and wigeon love to sport,
And duck and mallard oft resort,
Where wild-geese wet their pinions grey,
And stately herons love to stray;
There, o'er the shallow water's bed,
His baited hooks at eve he'd spread,
And leave them till the coming day,
  When flutt'ring o'er the ruffled tide,
The teal and wigeon strive in vain;

  And e'en the heron's crested pride
By the frail slender line is ta'en.

Various too, the snares he's spread
Where pheasants haunt the green wood shade:
Along their paths he'd lime-twigs lay,
Or spread the hair nooze in their way;
Or barley, oats, or wheat he'd use,
Steep'd in the Indian berry's juice,
Which, by the heedless birds devour'd,
Makes them fall senseless and o'erpowered,
At once a rich and easy prey:

X

Or, when at eve, amid the trees,
   The pheasants to their roost were gone,
And hush'd and still was every breeze;
   Oft would he seek the wood alone;
And 'neath some tree he'd take his stand,
A sulphur match light in his hand,
   When noxious vapours upwards thrown,
Thro' all the leaves and branches crept,
Stifling the pheasants as they slept.

Or in the dusk his snares he'd lay
   Within the entrance of some break,
There to remain till break of day,
   In hopes the timid hare to take:
Nor vain his hopes—for seldom he,
   When he revisited his snares,
Scarce ever failed at morn to see
   A hare reward his evening cares.

Such is the life that Hubert spends,
   Each night to lawless practice lent,
   Each day in low-liv'd pleasure spent
In some near pot house, with his friends;
Not like the friends which once he knew,
   When pass'd his days in honest toil;
But thieves and rogues, a drunken crew,
   Share in the product of his spoil;
While filthy jest, or obscure song,
All day the boisterous mirth prolong.

from *The Romance of Poaching*

"The blue heavens smiled, and the day was serene,
And a soft stillness lay on the dim moorland scene,
When a pilgrim I stood by the cairn on the heath,
Where Sandy the Poacher had breathed his last breath.

The prowess tradition delights to unfold
Of this marvellous poacher, so daring and bold,
Who his native integrity still could maintain,
And preserve a repute without blemish or stain.

No mean man, no rude skulking coward was he,
But noble and courteous, and brave as could be,
At the grand Ducal ball 'mong the noble and fair,
A welcome, as equal, brave Sandy had there.

A limb from his body had sooner been torn,
Than a wrong should for him by another be borne,
And to mortal more needful and poor than himself,
Right free would he part with his game or his pelf.

His fine spirit wounded, perchance he did leave
The haunts where men scramble, and cheat, and deceive,
And took his lone way to the mountain and wild,
To sojourn with Nature, her free, fearless child.

For years on the moors, from the Dee to the Spey,
He rested by night, and he wandered by day,
Till at last on the slope of the steep Craigenscore,
He sank on the heather to wander no more.

Ah! meet that the heather he loved so to tread,
The soft fragrant heather should be his death-bed,
And meet that his dog, constant comrade and true,
Should from his pale forehead lick off the death-dew.

True heart; from the story and kindly-kept cairn,
The worldly, the proud, and self-seeking may learn,
What it is gives a true lasting title to fame;
And long be remembered and honoured the name."

Ferret at work

Frontispiece: Caught poaching!

Boyhood
Memories

1

Figure 1.1 My main friends were dogs, my father knew a lot about dogs.

BOYHOOD MEMORIES

FORMATIVE YEARS

When I was still a boy at school, my greatest interests were always in the countryside. From the time I was able to take care of myself a little, I would be off fishing in some pond or wandering about the countryside. Wandering in the countryside by night or day was far more interesting to me than any of a town's artificial pleasures. Having a sleep under a dry hedge or by a warm stack was nothing to me. Even as a boy I fished in private pools and lakes at night-time and, somehow, never felt scared of the night sounds. In fact, by being out at night-time one learns a lot about the sounds of wildlife. The wild flowers, the woods, the wild birds and animals of the countryside have always held an interest for me.

There were many times that I have been miles from home at day-break, having wandered across country throughout the night. All this walking and wandering built up a good knowledge of the short cuts through the woods and the interiors of big estates. In later years, I often poached alone, even on the big keepered estates. Among all the various poachers that I ever got to know in a long life, I never met one who knew more about our own county than I did. There is not one estate in this area that I have not poached on at one time or another.

I always call my county the forgotten county, because very few writers write about North Staffordshire. They seem to think it is a drab area of factories and coal mines. They are very wrong because there are places here comparable to any in England for their beauty; there are some lovely spots hidden away in our countryside.

While I was still a schoolboy, I was taught how to make nets. By continual practice, I learned how to make all kinds of nets for game, birds or fish. Since those days, I have taught a few other poachers how to make their own nets, and, believe me, there is a great difference between a well made, hand knitted net and those bought from net firms.

During all my walking, I had a good memory for the places I had seen and what they held in the way of rabbits and other game. In later years, this knowledge was to prove the difference between success or failure as a poacher. I have met and worked with some good poachers, but I always found them to concentrate on one or two places only. I have been able to change places by as much as sixty miles when things got too hot at any one place. It has given me many a laugh when other poachers tried to guess where I had been working when I had a good haul.

MY ANIMAL FRIENDS

With regard to pets, the only pets that I ever kept were dogs and ferrets. Occasionally, I kept a few wild birds, a legal practice in those days. I found that the best ferrets came from the gamekeepers, who bred and trained them. My favourite dog was always a crossbred greyhound; greyhound and collie for preference, although other crosses are sometimes good. The fastest lurcher of all is a cross of greyhound and whippet, but, with their smooth coats, they are too vulnerable to injury. A cross greyhound and collie has speed, strength, and sense. My father knew a lot about dogs and I followed his advice, but his interest was in racers. He was so particular in his judgment of a dog that, even if the only fault lay in the tail not being dead centre and straight, he would

Figure 1.2 **Ferret.**

4

turn it down. He said a straight tail mattered a lot in racing dogs. Following his advice, I did not go in for any sort of dog that came along.

I really enjoyed and loved to train lurchers and, as a boy, I had some happy hours on moonlit nights. Using ferrets and a good lurcher on small sandy warrens can provide some really hectic sport on such nights. Also, good sport can be had by taking a dog out in open country. By the time I was fourteen to fifteen years old, I could handle dogs and ferrets to good purpose. Along with a friend of mine we had as many as twelve ferrets between us, along with good dogs. There were two other things my father told me — watch a dog's back legs when he walks and, if the legs go inwards, it is a sign of inbreeding. The next was never to have fighting dogs because they can lead to too much trouble. I am sure that the lurchers I had equally enjoyed every hour of their training, and they learn quickly that their job is illegal. A good, well-trained lurcher will soon let you know if anyone else is about!

From my boyhood studies of the wild birds, I turned my attentions to ferrets and rabbits. I felt a proud boy when I took home any rabbits that I had caught, as they were very useful to a large family. I carried on the game of ferrets and dogs for all it was worth, and I got into all sorts of trouble.

AN EARLY ARREST

I was first caught poaching with ferrets when I was a little over thirteen years old. This was quite by accident. There had been some robberies in a country village and the police were combing the fields in an effort to find the culprits. I was picked up and, of course, taken to a police station. After a lot of questions by the police sergeant, the farmer whose land I had been trespassing on was sent for. Seeing that I was only a boy, he refused to make any case of it, and, after a good lecture on the errors of what I was doing, I was set free. I made my way straight back to the fields and I had the good fortune to recover my two ferrets and nets. Throughout my life, I did not like to be known as a deserter of either dog, ferret or man when I was out on the poaching game.

Soon after this little incident, I got into trouble due to fishing in a private pond at night-time. In this case, I got a good beating by one of the men who were looking after the area, and my fishing tackle was smashed up into the bargain. My father was all for causing trouble over this affair, because I had several bruises; he was a big strong man who knew a little of 'Queensbury rules'. He could fight, and there would have been more trouble from the police. He was persuaded out of it by me telling him I would get the score even as time went on in my own way.

MOONLIGHT FORAYS

First I proceeded to catch some rabbits by moonlight ferreting, and 'Lady Luck' smiled. The chosen place had a lot of small sandy warrens on bank sides and they were ideal for moonlight work. This was where a good lurcher was very useful, and the dog I had at that time would soon give a warning if anything was amiss. I did very well off this area; I think the two men who were looking after it realised what was happening as the rabbits were being thinned out. I was one of those blamed for this, but guessing and proof are two very different things.

I was warned to keep off this place for a time to allow things to go quiet. I therefore moved to other areas, as I had by no means forgotten the beating I had received. So, after a time, a few ducks began to disappear. Raw liver and lob worms on fish hooks can be deadly for ducks. No one ever seemed to realise what had happened to them. Possibly, the foxes were blamed, but I really got it in the neck at home for this trick from my parents. I think they were a bit panicky about my own safety, and also the penalties would have been heavy. The evidence of feathers has to be burned and my family were really upset about the risk of it all. My parents never interfered with any dog or ferrets that I decided to keep, but felt this was going a bit too far.

FIRST INTRODUCTION TO SNARES

It was about this time that I came across a lot of rabbits in snares. I was out fishing one night on a private lake about eight miles from home. At intervals, I could hear the squeal of rabbits as they were getting caught in the snares, and being unable to resist the temptation of easy game, I had a few of those rabbits — what I could carry in a bag. If I was a long way from home at night-time, I used to catch the early morning trains or public transport. This was how other night wanderers got back home.

This set me off on the tricks of using snares. It takes a great deal of study, the trial and error kind, to learn to use snares to good effect. It is not as easy as some people would try to make others believe. I have read books by various authors on country life but none of them have explained clearly how to set snares. I tried my hand at snaring in all sorts of places, under bushes, on gorse commons, and even in the woods, with all kinds of success and failure. After some practice with snares, I began to learn a little about the best places to use them. I began to take more interest in snares, and, on my travels in the countryside, when I came across any snares that had been set, I studied them. I soon began to tell the difference between those set by novice and expert.

The average novice will cut his main pegs from a hedge or wood, mostly from hazels. The expert made his pegs in a much quicker way

6

Figure 1.3   Wild duck may be caught in many different ways

from elderberry wood. When elderberry branches of 8 or 9 inches (203 or 229 mm) are used, they split easily and the resulting pegs are very hard. A novice will set his snares close to the burrows on the main runs. The expert sets well out on the runs where the rabbits would be travelling faster. Some trappers will occasionally put in a white peg and he will know how many snares are set on each side of the peg. The type of wood used for snares is very important. If wood from boxes, for example, is used, the rabbits will rarely face the snares — their noses are not merely ornaments. The same thing applies to smoking while setting snares; although I have seen this denied in a book about countryside sports, it is unlikely that rabbits will not be put off by the smell. Some of the best trappers I ever got to know would cover their hands in sand or soil to try and prevent the taint of tobacco. In one book about poachers, the author advised setting snares at a height of 4 inches (10 cm) and between the jumps. He would not catch many like this, but it is everyone to their own ideas; back to my early days.

Snaring hares

It was while I was using snares that I came across some hares. They were travelling under some fences from off the very place where I had received the good beating. I set some snares under these fences, slightly larger than if they were set for rabbits. The next morning, I had caught my first hare. In my excitement, I took the hare and left some snares still set. This was a bad mistake and one of the many lessons on careless poaching. The man who had beat me found those snares, although they were not actually on his property. I do not know if he found a rabbit in the snares, but I do know the kind soul who told him that I had sold a hare. I was reported to the police on the grounds that hares were on the game list. In due course, a warning was received from the police about my conduct. It was a case of enmity now because I never could accept good poaching as bad conduct. This was a frame of mind that I carried all through life.

DOG AND FERRET

After this little affair, I was breaking in a dog to ferrets and I came across a place where quite a number of rabbits had made their home. They were in some rocks at the side of a brickwork's marlpit. Ferrets and dogs were useless here, so it was back to my snares again. My snares were set in a meadow at the top of the marlpit where the rabbits were feeding. At daybreak the next morning, I was looking over my snares and I had got six rabbits, when I was surprised by the works' policeman. While he was trying to catch me, he put his foot in one of my snares and came a real cropper. I had lost my bag in the scramble and so I had to make my

Figure 1.7 Hare caught in a snare.

9

way through the brickworks carrying my rabbits openly. This policeman knew me and my family well and he came to see me at home. My father laughed at him with his threats and said; "Never mind the threats, old boy. You do have to catch him first." I was threatened with dire destruction if I had any more of what he called his rabbits. That same policeman was a big man and was one of our local boxers. He once challenged any man in the area to a boxing match. He thought he was too good to be beaten but the challenge was taken up by an ex-sailor. The sailor won the match. Boxing matches were quite common in those days.

A few years later, that same policeman thought he was clever. Instead of myself, he had arrested my younger brother for trespassing. It is said that police courts do not exact vengeance, but I do not believe it. He paid more for that than any of us who were poachers, even in later years.

GATE NETS

I next tried my hand at **gate netting** for hares. I had been listening to an old poacher talking to my father about these things. He was one of the old school of poachers and had been to prison a few times for poaching in his younger days. When I was a boy at school, he was sentenced to twelve months hard labour for stabbing a gamekeeper in a night affray. I well remember this affair, because his own boy was in the same class. In this fight, he killed a dog which the keepers tried to turn on him — he was a very cruel man to his dogs. Having poached on the same estate myself, many times as I got older, I can still recall him standing at a bedroom window with a double-barrelled gun threatening the police below. Such rough tactics do not pay in my own opinion, although there are others just as bad. This particular man ended his days in a mental home. He once did me a good turn, however, when I got into trouble for trespassing, 'trespass in pursuit of game' the police said it was. He moved my ferrets and tackle to his own home until the trouble passed over.

Poaching in those days was really hectic and one never knew where things would end if you were caught. Some magistrates were really heavy, especially if they happened to be landowners.

I made myself two gate nets of five yards each and also acquired a crossbred brindle greyhound. I was doomed to failure at this part of the game. Those hares would run anywhere except to my nets. The reason for this was that I was trying to catch them in open country, with open fences and hedgerows. Gate nets are almost useless unless the hedges are good and thick or one is working in stone wall country, such as the Derbyshire hills. It was another old poacher who explained to me the reasons for failure. I was also to learn that two men are best for this method, one at the net and the other one out with the dog. The object of

10

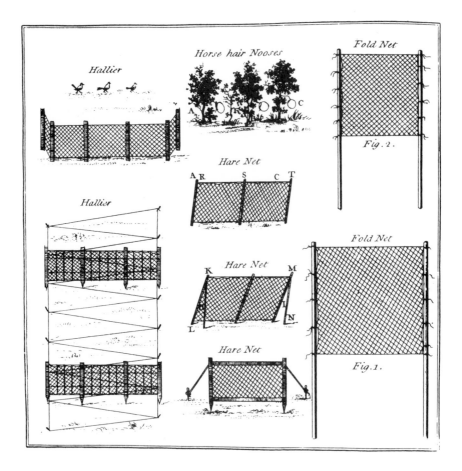

HARE-NETS AND RABBIT-NETS. The three several sorts of nets represented here, are proper either for hares or rabbits ... In the placing of these observe the path or track in any coppice, or furrow, which any hare uses to pass; likewise how the wind is ... if the wind be side-ways it will do well enough, but never let it blow over the net into the hare's face, for he will scent both it and you at a distance ... The net represented by the last figure is less troublesome than either of the former ... yet it is good only for rabbits and hares; whereas the others are useful also for the taking of wolves, foxes, badgers and pole-cats.

Figure 1.5 Old style nets. (From: *Sportsman's Dictionary*)

11

the dog is to keep the hare moving at speed.

One fault of hare poaching lies in the fact that gate nets can be set up and the hares will be somewhere else. It is a chancy business. On the subject of hares, some nature writers write a lot of of rubbish about them. They try to make people believe that hares cannot see directly to the front, and that their eyes are well back so that they can see behind them. I have seen hares turn from nets at no more than one or two feet if one of their kind has struck the net first. One further point, hares will not be caught in thick woodlands. They love the open spaces.

After these failures, I carried on with my **ferrets and dogs**. When I was about fifteen years old, I was out one night picking mushrooms off a place which was a little bit too hot to visit in the daytime. By being 'hot' I mean a place where someone is always on the lookout. It was here that I met a party of three men who were after rabbits with long nets. I happened to know these men, because they used to deal with my father for various tackle.

When these men came to my home, it was one question after another, to find out why and how these long nets were used. I was told a few elementary things, but that was all. I could make nets and so I decided to make my own and to teach myself the hard way. The tangles and troubles that I had were numerous until I finally got the hang of running out a net without too much trouble. I put in a lot of practice in the fields close to home. I was to learn that practising in daylight and working in the dark are not the same, but it gave one that vital feeling in the hands.

LONG NETS

The same author I have mentioned previously wrote in his book about poachers that it was not possible for one man to work long nets by himself. He is wrong. I have in my time caught hundreds of rabbits and hares by going out alone with a long net. There were, indeed, a lot of people who would not believe that I could work alone. As I got older and more experienced, I would rather use a long net for night poaching than any other method. It is the most humane method there is for killing game. Any that escape the nets or break free are not injured in any way. Believe me, it is a very skilled game to make it pay good dividends year after year. There is a great difference between netting two thousand or more in a season and what I used to get as a boy.

While I was still in my teens, I worked along with a boyhood friend who, I am glad to say, was a good friend from boyhood days to old age, except that he did not take to night poaching. Between us, by the time I was fifteen years old, we had as many as twelve ferrets plus dogs. There was plenty of work to do because we took up jobs of killing rats on farms and other places. Some of these jobs on farms were taken up in exchange for permission to catch some of the rabbits. There were some farmers who even then would not let us have the rabbits, and so we got them as often as possible by other methods. Where conditions suit, such as small sandy warrens, it is great fun in the moonlight with good dogs.

About this time, a young fellow came to see us. He said he was studying natural history and he asked us if we could get him some hedgehogs. A deal was made at a price of one shilling each (5np). One of our dogs was really good at finding hedgehogs. He would find the hedgehog and wait for us to pick it up. It did not take long to get a sackful of these; they were quite common. That young man had a surprise when they were duly delivered at his home. We did not get the one shilling each for all of them, because there were too many. We did not hear of that young man studying wild nature again! In case anyone has a laugh at these petty deals, they must bear in mind that this was in the days of real hardship.

Among the ferrets which passed through our hands was one of a chocolate colour. It was the only one I have ever seen of that colour, but he was useless for work. He would sit at the mouth of a burrow and would go back down the burrow if anyone tried to pick him up. We often had to resort to other tricks to catch him. No amount of training with

Figure 1.6 **Hedgehogs.** Supplying hedgehogs became a temporary source of income.

13

other ferrets did him any good. One day when we were out after rabbits, another man was along with us. He was using a twelve-bore gun. Eventually, this man lost his patience and shot our chocolate ferret. There were no regrets; it was probably the best end of a nuisance.

RATTING

Ratting with ferrets and dogs is good sport but, believe me, ferrets do not get things all their own way among rats. Sometimes they are badly mauled and injured. One farmer asked us to clean up some rats for him and, when we went to the farm there were pens of turkeys being fattened up ready for the markets. He assured us that they were quite safe because all holes in the brickwork had been sealed up. Unfortunately, one of our ferrets broke through a hole which was only covered by a thin shale of cement. He really made the feathers fly, and he had killed two of those young turkeys before we could get the farmer to open the doors. Luckily, he was a decent sort of farmer and there were no grumbles.

Another farm that we went to belonged, in part, to an ex-army officer. He was very keen on shooting and he asked us to allow him to have some sport shooting the rats. We were working on some small stacks and, when the rats began to bolt, it was like a bombardment. He was very excitable and ended up killing two of our ferrets. He was like someone who had gone berserk and was shooting as soon as he saw a rustle in the straw. I think he would have shot at anything that moved, including our dogs, if we had let them loose. I was glad when that visit was over, and, needless to say, we did not visit that farm again.

On another occasion, we were after the rabbits at a country place known to us as the 'Manor' and we lost one of our ferrets — a black fitchet. He was a big, strong ferret and had escaped from his box. He found his way to the local vicarage and another small farm where he did some damage killing poultry and ducks. There was quite a big outcry over this affair, mainly from the vicar. That vicar called in the police as though it was a murder case. We strongly denied ownership of that ferret because we could not have paid for the damage.

One day when we were out rat-killing on some corn stacks, we met quite a character of an old man, a farm hand. Corn threshing was in progress and we had set long nets between the stacks to prevent the rats crossing over. What amused me was the way this old man could handle a pitchfork. If a rat moved and it was anywhere within his striking distance, he could pierce it like lightning with the prong of his pitchfork. I never saw him miss while I was watching him. The long stack nets which were used for rats were my own, made on the same lines as the rabbit nets but in $1\frac{1}{4}$ inch (3 cm) mesh. It takes a long time and a lot of work to make nets like these but they were useful. The real excitement came as the stacks came to the bottom.

DRAGNETTING PARTRIDGES

There are no corn stacks in this modern age; it is baling machines or combine harvesters now. At home, I was listening to a man talking about dragnetting for skylarks. My father was not a poacher, and never had been, but he was a tackle and cage-maker. The keeping of cage birds was quite common in those days and skylarks were among the top favourites. My father would not tackle the job of knitting a long drag net because they take too long to make, and neither would I make one for someone else. After further discussion, I decided to make one for myself as this was also the method of netting partridges. Drag nets are expensive and almost impossible to buy. I made the net twenty-five yards long and four yards deep. These nets are made in $1\frac{1}{4}$ inch (3 cm) square mesh and so it took a long time to make it. A strong rope line is threaded round the entire net with two pull lines at the top corners of the net.

Some men put weights at the back with the idea of keeping the net down to the ground. This is not necessary and is noisy. The noise upsets the birds and they rise before the net reaches them. I did my first drag-netting for larks in the company of a friend of mine. It was while we were out after larks together that we captured our first covey of partridges. We were netting on a dry meadow and, by sheer luck, those partridges happened to be right in the centre of the net and we caught eight of them. I was to learn later that when using a drag net, if one of the men upsets the birds by walking into them, keep quiet for a short while and they can be picked up in ones and twos. Anyone who lives in the countryside can mark down partridge at dusk. They will be heard calling to each other as they settle down for the night.

Netters should always try to work with the wind on the 'shoulder' and, if stubble fields are worked, pick a night of fairly strong wind. It is surprising what can be picked up with a drag net in the early season. About August, anyone working on keepered estates would almost certainly pick up some of the young pheasants. Contrary to the opinion of many so-called naturalists, pheasants do not take to the trees until later in the year, after their first moult. Any gamekeeper knows that before the first moult is a very dangerous time for pheasants from foxes.

Anyone who thinks or gives their opinion that dragnetting is easy should have a go at it; they will find it very hard work, especially in hilly country. The only country suitable for dragnetting is where the fields are clean and clear of obstructions such as thistles, bushes, and so on. Gamekeepers will often stake out bushes on meadowlands. I used to be very fond of dragnetting, but I was soon to learn that the monetary rewards at this game are not to be compared with the money to be

Figure 1.7 Dragnetting partridges. These nets take a long time to make

Figure 1.8 Skylark, popular cage birds of old, which also fell victim to the drag net.

16

earned out of rabbits. One can get into more trouble for the sale of one pheasant or partridge than for the sale of a hundred rabbits. The game laws are soon brought down on anyone selling feathered game.

GROWING INTERESTS

When I was about eighteen years old, a relative of mine got into trouble. While I was at work, he had taken out my ferrets and my dog, a crossbred greyhound, without my permission. He finished the day with the loss of three ferrets and several nets, and was later fined heavily at the local police court. The local police even tried to have my dog destroyed and this led to nasty quarrels both with the one who had caused the trouble and my own family for allowing him to take my belongings. The police were told they were going too far and they had no authority to destroy my dog. My ferrets had been replaced but they were young ones who needed training all over again. It seems one of those curious things in life but this same man often caused me trouble in the poaching game in later years. This affair put the police on my track, but I refused to be bluffed by them and I began to take more interest in night poaching. There was a far greater thrill in night poaching and all through life I always loved a night out. I was now beginning to get really handy with a long net and I was catching far more game than any daylight work. All kinds of tricks were used to get the catch home if I was working any distance from home.

AN ECONOMIC NECESSITY

There was not much work to be had in those days and there was plenty of time to study the countryside and its wildlife. I knew my way about for miles around and, when one place failed or got upset, I moved on to another. When I say that I knew my way about, I mean in the fields and woods, and the large estates; the way the different brooks and streams would lead and the rides in the woods and where they would lead to. Believe me, knowledge of the countryside at night-time is an education in itself. It is all very easy in the daytime, but very few people have a good sense of direction in the night. When there was no work, I was hardly ever at home. I was always game for any poaching mischief or trespassing in search of more knowledge. Apart from my love of poaching, I kept my character clean and this was to prove a very good thing in later life.

I was to find that the continual walking and hunting in the country was to gain me very useful knowledge in later life. Please bear in mind, anyone who reads this, that these were hard years. Poverty was widespread in this country for a good many years, thus I was always

17

Figure 1.9   Pheasants, a prime target.

trespassing and trying to gain more knowledge of every estate that I knew.

I have got out of a good many tight corners due to this knowledge. Some poachers used to say that I tried to know too much countryside, but I have never been at a loss for some place to go to if I wanted any game. Another thing that I learned was the fact that the more the estates were keepered the better for the poacher who dared to go on them. This does not mean that plenty of game could not be caught off other lands. I was beginning to study things more closely, as to why one field would catch game and another one would fail. The wind, of course, was only one of the answers to this and it takes a good poacher to know in advance where the wind would strike any particular wood, hedgerow or burrow.

Figure 2. The Manor House — the grounds provided fine poaching

I Become an Experienced Poacher

2

Figure 2.1 My poaching skills soon came to match those of the fox.

I BECOME AN EXPERIENCED POACHER

EMERGING AS A LEADER

My early youth was behind me and I was now an experienced and accomplished poacher. I have heard a good many poachers talk about what they know, but let them go out alone and one will soon see what they can really do. All my life I have only known four men who tried to poach alone. By this time, I was getting to be well known to other men who used to try a spot of poaching. I have heard more than one older man say, "What does he know, he is only a boy yet." Time was to prove these things. By this time, I could hold my own with any poachers that I knew and the jealousies that flared up were numerous. Some of them tried to question me about the various places, and some of the rougher men threatened to cut my nets and so on. I was never daunted by any man's threats and I carried on the night poaching game for a lifetime, until 'Father Time' called a halt to it. In all those years, the only net I ever lost was one which the police confiscated when I was prosecuted for poaching on a big estate near Market Drayton. This happened in 1930.

ENCOUNTER WITH KEEPERS

I have, of course, had a good many narrow escapes from both police and keepers. One narrow escape, which I well remember, happened on an estate in the west of our county. I had come across an old haystack and loose wood which had been piled up together. A good number of rabbits were under this and I had set some snares. It was not suitable for the net. When I went to look at my snares in the early morning, the keepers were waiting for me. As I drew near to the place on my cycle, I saw the sun glint on a gun barrel. Instead of turning back, I passed close by the man with the gun lying in some bushes. I bid him, "Good morning, sir." What would I have given for a camera at that moment! Both keepers came out of their hiding places and began swearing at me. I stood there in all my innocence and asked what was wrong. The only thing wrong that I could see was that they had some rabbits out of my

23

snares. I got to know both of those keepers in later years. I do not know what they would have said if I had been caught after the pheasants. At various times, I have poached all over their area at night-time.

The Informer

It is surprising if you are a known poacher what other people will try to do against you. They do not have the nerve or knowledge to do anything like this themselves, but they will take care that all they see is passed on to the police. I well remember one young fellow about my own age who was supposed to be a Scout leader. He was one of the kind always on the lookout for something to report to the police, and was once praised for his public spirit, when he had informed on some petty gamblers. He also informed the police of my selling of rabbits, and so on. When I did corner him, I paid him out with my fists. It was very fortunate that I was not prosecuted for it. This was the same person I have mentioned earlier. I hate informers and squealers and yet one meets them all the way through life.

THE HUNGRY YEARS

My family began to break up and I left home when I was twenty-two years old. The poverty and degradation among the working class of that time was a national disgrace. I do not care what others think of me for what I have done, but my poaching skills found good dinners for a good many people. Work was very scarce and men were working naked on a coal face for as little as seven shillings (35np) per day, and an average of three days per week. I did not intend that I should go hungry or short of money if I could prevent it, and so I pushed on with the night poaching. In the way of economics, on a decent night, I could earn more than a full week at work; but it must be borne in mind that poaching cannot be carried out night after night. I always had a ready market for my catch among my own work friends.

I sometimes worked along with other poachers. They did not have the knowledge of the countryside as I knew it. Their knowledge of the countryside covered that which was close to home, and what I knew farther afield began to prove its worth. Some of these men were a lot older than myself and they remained my friends to the end of their days. There were also, however, other so-called poachers who began to realise that I knew something about the game and jealousies often flared up into quarrels and threats. Like every other aspect of life, there was good and bad. Among the bad ones were those who would use poor nets because they would not pay the price of good ones. Also, they could not make their own. In the event of trouble, they would desert their nets and stand to lose very little. They thought more about their own skins and are best left out of this game.

Figure 2.2   An old style gamekeeper and his dog, an industrious race but best avoided by poachers.

THE BUNGLERS

Among the unwritten rules of poachers is the rule that, if you meet in the night you either go your different ways or work together. This is an experience I once had. I was out alone and met two men who were using one net. I knew one of them and it was decided that we should work together. After two sets, I realised they were using a bad net. Out of sixty odd rabbits snared, they had caught only one. I did not inform them that I had arranged for a friend of mine to pick me up in the morning. When the car came, I left them with the one rabbit and their bad net. Another one of this kind I met one night had had his net thrown onto a thorn bush, and he was left to try and get it off himself.

By this time, I did not need either dogs or ferrets. I could do better without a dog. Any reader of this may smile, but a box of matches half full was better than a dog for beating to the nets.

Once, in the early twenties, I had a night out with two men who were supposed to be good poachers. We were working on a big parkland. I was very surprised at their methods. They would set their nets anywhere, regardless of wind, methods of approach or gates. I was disgusted and I told them so, but they would not listen to me. The total catch for three men was seven rabbits. We had travelled by train to a country station and they said they knew the way back. Their way was miles out and, from where we were, the distance to the station was two miles. This is where good knowledge of the country is invaluable.

FRIENDS ON THE RAILWAY

I never went out in their company again. By this time I was getting well known to the police. Several of the poachers I knew were arrested, mostly as they were on their way home. I remember two who had seven convictions, all for poaching. In one case, the police were waiting for us outside a railway station. One of the poachers' wives was on the station to warn us that someone had been informing about us. We travelled on to the next station, where I knew the station master. That cargo of rabbits and nets was duly delivered to my home inside the hour by the railway van while we went home empty-handed. The railway people were very good to us in those days. Some of them would go out of their way to help us. At various places well out in the country we had friends on the railways. One such was a linesman who used to leave us a key and coal for a fire in case the nights were wet or cold. At this same country station we sometimes sent the nets out by rail, in a flat basket. They would be picked up at the station, and next morning rabbits and nets would be packed in the basket and sent home.

This linesman was a really good man to know and, of course, we left him a dinner if we were working in that area. Many people do not know that county police cannot do as they like on railway property. It is classed as private land. This was proved one morning at a certain country railway station. There had been a change of staff and the new station master was an arrogant snob. Three of us had about ninety rabbits that morning and he refused to allow us to take them on the train. Instead, he telephoned for the policeman who lived nearby. He came down to us and examined what we had. His answer was, "No feathers. Looks as if you have had a good night boys. I'll have a couple off you. How much do you want?" He then told me he was not in a position to do anything on railway property because they had their own police for such matters. That country policeman never did arrest us, although he sometimes had the chance. He was a good sort of policeman; one of the champion heavyweight boxers of the force.

ADVENTURES

One one occasion, three of us were out and we were doing quite well until we came to cross a main road. One of my friends opened the field gate quietly to make sure the road was clear. As we stepped into the road, two policemen revealed themselves. One of them was our policeman friend. We had about forty rabbits which would have been left for picking up in the morning by car. After a routine check-up, one of them said, "Come along and bring those rabbits with you to the police station." We fully expected that it would be a prosecution case, and so all nets and the rabbits were put on the roadside. We had finished work for that night and the policemen were invited to carry their own evidence if it was to be a prosecution. The policeman's own home was under a mile away and the police station was three miles away. This action was no more than cheeky bluff and they knew it. They could have taken us away without the evidence. After some arguing, they said, "Well, we will let you go for now and catch you some other time." That ended that small incident but it had spoiled the rest of the night. That policeman always had our respect after that.

In this same area of country, we were working along a valley following the course of the river. There were a lot of big sandy warrens along the valley. Suddenly, we were jumped by three more poachers who had come on the job too late. They thought they would frighten us off and steal our catch. It did not work as they thought and, in the scuffle, two of them were knocked clean into the river. We knew these men and we spread the word around to others that they must have been in need of a bath. They did not try that trick on us again.

I was once puzzled by the rabbits in a big wood in this area. I knew they were there in good numbers but we could never catch more than a few at a time. I found out the reason for this quite by accident. I was listening to a conversation in a country inn between farm hands and some shooting men. These rabbits were travelling to a large area which had been allowed to go rough. On this area were a lot of wild weeds, and rabbits, like birds, love weeds. After that, they were easy to catch by setting the nets behind the hedges instead of on the woodside, a method known to us as 'back hedging'. They were often left until well into the night to allow them to travel well out from the woods.

As time went on, that area was practically cleaned out, although the rabbits soon multiplied again. Also, it was getting too well known to other poachers. That was not the only place to be thinned out of rabbits in that district, and it led to a lot of enmity between farmers, keepers and poachers. Over thirty years after these episodes, if I called in at that village inn, someone would mention the poachers. This village inn was also used by our linesman friend and he always treated me openly. He used to say that he was amazed to know that I was the ringleader, although I was the youngest. He used to say, "Although you have done a lot of poaching, I admire you for your nerve and courage." Early one morning, our linesman friend watched us load up 196 rabbits into a car. One farmer in this part of the country threatened what he would do if he caught me. I do not like threats of violence and his place which had several woods got a real hammering. Sometimes two pairs of netters

Figure 2.3 Rabbits provided the main spoils from a night's poaching.

28

would be at work on each side of his land and working to the centre. We always carried powerful flashlights to warn each other if anything went wrong. It was off his land that we had the 196 mentioned above. They do not last long at this rate of killing. The biggest problem with hauls like this is getting them to a suitable loading point. More than one journey has to be made.

There was one man in this area who did some trapping and ferreting for the local farmers and he had a very strong dislike of poachers. He had a mongrel dog which he thought was good. Probably he was to ferrets, I do not know. I was having a country ride with a friend of mine in his car. He owned a really good lurcher, a leggy rough-haired greyhound type of dog. I took the dog into the Inn as though it was my own property. By the scowls on that man's face, I think he would have shot that dog and myself as I was praising what that dog would do. I did this to torment this man on the spur of the moment. The owner of that dog was a telephone linesman and the dog was always in his van. It was as my friend said; there were plenty of opportunities for the dog.

OLD BILL

The railway linesman I have written about lived to a good age but he ended his days suffering from several years of total blindness. About four or five miles from the area I have been writing about lived a really good trapper and I have had some happy times in his company. He taught me quite a lot about snaring and gin trapping. When I was out trapping with this man, I had ample opportunity to look round various places and very often those rabbits which were not set to him to trap were poached at night-time by nets. He knew that I was poaching at night-time when I had the chance but he always trusted me to leave his traps and snares alone, and this I always did.

There was one thing wrong with this man, he was of a very happy nature and was easily put on. Some country people were always trying to beg rabbits and other game off him instead of paying a fair price. I have seen boxes in his shed at home with snares, purse nets, string and wire, and money all mixed up together. He did not value money. I often used to tease him a little about his appearance. He was the very image of that war-time character, Bruce Bairnsfather's "Old Bill". Nothing ever seemed to upset him.

STOATS

He had a real knowledge of country life and he taught me more than one sharp lesson about wildlife. One day we were trapping on some big sandy warrens in a valley. As we were setting the traps, stoats were seen

29

Figure 2.4 Stoats track down rabbits with great skill

Figure 2.5 The badger, often a nuisance to the poacher.

30

moving about in the grass. He said that we may be in for trouble and the next morning some of these stoats were in the traps. I asked him for those stoats in order to skin them. There were always advertisements about for skins of all kinds. He just grinned and told me to take them. I took out my knife and began to skin one. There was a terrible stench and it made me sick. When I had recovered he told me never to try to skin a stoat unless it had been hung in the open air for a day at least. It is this stench which leads some naturalists to think that stoats use this stench when hunting. My trapper friend told me that when stoats die they throw off a kind of vapour.

There is one great fallacy about stoats which a good many people still believe, that when any rabbit or hare hears or sees a stoat, they lie down and squeal in terror. If this were true, how does anyone account for it when stoats can be seen to cross fields and there will be scores of rabbits about. How nice it would be if one could come across a field with a hundred petrified rabbits just because a stoat is about. I have been watching the movements of rabbits to see which way they are running and have actually seen stoats pass by into the woods and the rabbits have not taken any notice. It is mostly in the winter months or late autumn that stoats will kill rabbits. Even then, they do not go for the old bucks or old does. The stoat is a very persistent trailer and will trail the fresh scent of his quarry for a long time until he wears him down. When countryside walkers hear the squeal of a rabbit attacked by a stoat, or see a stoat on his kill, they are witnessing the end of a long chase. I have stood on high vantage points such as high bridges and watched these happenings. I have watched a stoat's final run on his quarry and that run has covered three fields, before he made his first strike at the rabbit. When that stoat was running flat out, he looked twice his normal size.

An interesting thing to watch is a stoat pack when they are training their young. The parents will be seen to weave in and out of rough places and along hedgerows and the young ones will be heard chattering away as they tumble along. It is not often that anyone will see a stoat kill a rabbit in the spring months when rabbits are breeding. The does will fight and defend their young just as other animals will. I have seen doe rabbits hook stoats up in the air with their back legs and sometimes the terrific blow is fatal. This is not always the case but I have seen doe rabbits kill stoats. Who can understand the workings of wild nature? It is all very nice for so-called nature writers to write about these things. There is a lot that is written that is wrong and there is a lot to be learned.

SKINNING A BADGER

It was this same trapper who set me to work to skin a badger. What a filthy greasy job this is. There is a thick layer of fat under the skin of a badger which has to be removed with a knife. It is a slow and dirty job. I think he did this with me to teach me what the job was like, more so than his interest in the value of the skin. Needless to say, I never again tried to skin a badger. To skin a fox, cat, rabbit or hare is child's play compared to the badger.

Badgers are night wanderers, 'nocturnal' like some other wild creatures, but I know for a fact that they are more common than some people think.

Badgers are rarely seen by people who lie in bed. I could name a lot of places that had badgers. At least, this was so in my poaching years when I travelled the country a lot. On one of our trips, one very large badger had the misfortune to get in front of our car when we were on our way home after a night's poaching. He was dead when I got out of the car, and I put him on the roadside. This happened near what is now the big Blithfield reservoir at Abbotts Bromley. Do not believe all that may be read about how clean 'Brock' is. I have had them on several occasions running into my nets and I can assure anyone that the smell from them is awful. I once hung my nets out to dry after having tangled with two badgers and my neighbours complained of a bad smell. They did not know the cause of it, but after that, if I had any trouble with badgers, the nets were soaked in soapy water.

Badgers have a habit of scraping out such places as fox earths or anywhere else where rubbish collects, as well as their own earths. It is this which leads some of our nature writers to say this is their habit of being clean. In my own humble opinion, for what it is worth, it is their hunting for food such as worms and beetles. Badgers will dig out young rabbits if they are close to the surface and they will also eat carrion. Badgers can be snared with steel wire on their runs but they are dangerous customers if the snare does not do its work properly.*

TRAPPING

During the time I was with my trapper friend, a man from the South came to live in the same district. He had been an underkeeper and, to hear him talk, he was going to catch everything that was wild. Where he came from, no poacher had a chance to get away with anything. The keepers down there were too clever for poachers, so he said. He had his first lesson on a big farm where he had taken up the trapping rights. He caught up the rabbits or he thought he had. A few weeks later, my friend had permission from the farmer to follow up on the rabbits and in one night about 200 were caught by snares. I worked along with and did

*Badgers are now protected by law. It is illegal to take or kill badgers without a special licence. This section was written before the act was passed.

carrying of the snares for him. There was also another man from the village setting snares along with him and he was a good snarer too. The total catch of that day's snaring was about 300 because they are not all snared in the first night. A year or two later, he was taught something about poachers and poaching.

My old trapper friend explained methods of trapping to me. Where the ex-underkeeper had gone wrong was in using steel traps in the first place instead of snares first and traps second. My friend always maintained that a lot of rabbits will not face steel traps and this was the reason a lot of them are left underground. If this is the general rule, I do not know, but I had another similar experience with him on another farm. We had been working on some sandy warrens, one of which was a narrow strip. All the holes were filled in as the traps were taken out and yet two weeks later we had a further 80 rabbits out of that strip of sand.

MOLEY JACK

In this countryside, I came to know a real specimen of a countryman. He was known as 'Moley Jack' because he was a mole trapper. He was six feet three in his socks and as straight as a Guardsman. In fact, he was an ex-Guardsman. I never knew him to ride anything, not even a bicycle. Ten to twenty miles on 'Shanks pony' was nothing to him and to cross the countryside with him was a killing exercise. What he did not know about that countryside was very little. As we got more friendly, he was a veritable mine of information about rabbits, game, fishing and keepers. He was a countryman from head to toe and was great friends with the trapper friend of mine. He told me a lot about the various types of people such as farmers and landowners in those areas. Just as in other walks of life, there are good and bad and some of them were on the mean side. Some of them are too mean and greedy to allow anyone else to live.

I used to love to poach the rabbits and other game from these areas. One farmer in particular was a real nuisance. He was always carrying his gun and threatened anyone who even looked at his place. He was involved in prosecutions against people who took mushrooms or watercress off his land.

He had a nice lot of rabbits in an open fence of hawthorn facing his farmhouse. One day, when it was a bit misty, I took a chance and set some snares along this fence. The two elderly trappers seemed quite upset when I informed them of what I had done. I was sure to get shot they said. Anyhow, I had a nice haul out of the snares and got them away to a cottage in the village. In an escapade like this, some of the snares are bound to be left behind and these would cause an upset to that farmer. During this little affair, done mostly in cheek, I spotted some goldfinches feeding on the thistles. The goldfinches were great favourites among

33

bird keepers. I told a certain person of what I had seen and that same relative I have mentioned previously for losing my ferrets got to know. He did a little bit more interfering and he went after those goldfinches. The result was that the police and the farmer whose rabbits I had taken arrested him. He duly appeared at the County police court and was fined very heavily, perhaps with a little bit of vengeance thrown in for me. Who knows? I still believe that Courts do take vengeance, in spite of all their denials. Even in those days the goldfinches were on the protected list. This person I have mentioned had the audacity to ask me to help him to pay his fines out of the rabbits I had taken. This to me was sublime cheek, and he was told that mistakes have to be paid for. My two old friends often had a laugh over that affair.

A good many of that mean farmer's rabbits were taken by night netting. One day a son of his accused me of being responsible for night setting. It was in the village inn that he started the trouble. He was, of course, quite correct, but I was not inclined to be browbeaten by him. Outside, a fight started up but it did not last long as I was well able to take care of myself in those days. I had no more trouble with him after that.

Figure 2.6 The goldfinch, at one time caught by bird fanciers but now protected by law.

LOCAL GENTRY

It was in this same village inn that a well-dressed gentleman started a conversation about wildlife such as concerned farmers, landowners, sportsmen, gamekeepers, poachers and others. Along with the other men, I was drawn into the discussion and at times it got a little heated as the various views were put forward. One of the older men whispered to me who the man was. He was one of our best known Lords and he owned a very large and beautiful estate. Someone mentioned poachers to him and told him that I was one of them. He was very interested in this part of the conversation and he admitted that he did not have the slightest knowledge of how poachers worked. I did not intend to tell him about the game, but he was told that I knew every wood, copse, pool and warren on his large estate. He was a very nice gentleman and he often came into the bar room to have a drink with the locals when he had been out trout fishing. He also had a great respect for the village people. I never told him how many times I had poached on his estate. That would not do. That lovely estate I am very sorry to say does not exist now as a game preserve. It was broken up during the last big war and nothing has been done by the government to put this land back to farming. Poacher or not, I love to see lovely places such as this was and I would not cause damage except by poaching.

The easy-going, happy nature of my trapper friend can be realised by the fact that a dealer once approached him for his rabbits and a good amount of money was owing. He did not even know who that dealer was, but I did. When it was realised that the money was not forthcoming, two of us took the matter into our own hands. We went to the man's shop, ten miles away, and I told him that I was the trapper's son. I demanded immediate payment or I would tell the people in that shop what kind of man he was. He tried to bluster his way out, he was coming to pay and so on, but I had that money. When that dealer was told he had been beaten at his game, he even threatened to prosecute me for false statements. He did not try any more tricks like that and other farmers and trappers were warned about his methods of non-payment. 'Moley Jack' had a good chuckle over this affair of getting the money back.

THE RIDE NET

It was in the company of these two characters that I first saw a **ride net** used in the daytime. They asked me to make one for them and I set to work to make it. I made it eight yards long in $1\frac{1}{2}$ inch square (4 cm) mesh. It is very slow work to make these nets by hand but there was some fun when it was made and ready for use. My friends knew how to use ride

35

Figure 2.7 Fine examples of Staffordshire country houses; their estates provided hunting for the gentry as well as ample game for the poacher. Many have now gone.

nets. The keeper on a certain estate some miles from the village was away for some reason and these two had the rabbit and mole trapping to do and they had the place to themselves.

The net was set about fifteen yards inside a dark ride and then a period of time was given for the woods to settle down again. It is surprising what disturbance is caused when one enters a wood. All the inhabitants of a wood seem to be on the edge of a panic. After a time, one of them circled the wood and entered the ride at the opposite end. Making a bit of noise he began beating to the hanging net.

I have seen in books that ride nets are not very successful, but this is not quite true. I will try to explain their failings or faults a little later. That net was catching all kinds of birds that flew down that ride. Pigeons, magpies, blackbirds, and pheasants were all victims to that net, but one does not kill the unwanted birds. It is of course a very dangerous game in the daytime because these nets cannot be moved in a hurry if the poaching is disturbed. The secret of them is to set the net in a dark ride where the trees are thick and facing the open fields. The fields are light in comparison to the woods and all birds when disturbed make for the light area. I can still remember their grinning faces over that net. They told me it was partly a lesson to show me something and partly because they did not get on very well with the gamekeeper on the estate. That net did its work in a few woods in that area, very often where there were no gamekeepers. Eventually we got too cheeky, we ran into trouble and had to leave it to its fate. The failings of these nets from a poacher's point of view is that special places have to be picked out with convenient branches to tie the net up to. It is obvious that they cannot be moved in a hurry. They are also useless on thin woods or commons, and the time it takes to free small birds is wasted time.

OTTER HUNTING

One day, I was out with my two old friends and I was intent on watching an otter hunt which was in progress. Hunting indeed, the row they made was enough to frighten anything within yards! The men and youths were as excited as the dogs. Up the river they went, yelling and yapping, smacking at the weed-beds and some of them in the water poking under the banks with long sticks and yelling like wild Indians. They were making their way up river to a big mill pool where otters had been seen. When they were out of sight 'Moley Jack' asked me what I thought about it. He said he could see that I was disgusted.

I told him that none of my boyhood lurchers would have made that noise. Giving me his usual sly grin, he took me to a bed of large stones and thick weed in a back water well off the main stream. It was the sight of a lifetime, the otter was lying very still between two large stones.

Figure 2.8 Otter hunting, now an illegal sport in England and Wales.

When he saw that we had found him, he made off downstream. He was lovely to watch as he took a dive into the main stream. I looked at my friends and wondered how they both had known that the otter would be lying in that bed and yet they did not inform that hunting party. Their thoughts were probably like mine, that it was very poor sport. I had more fun and excitement on moonlight nights in my boyhood days with my lurchers than all those so-called hunters. A good many fishermen hate otters, mostly the 'high brow' troutmen, but to me they are too lovely to kill for killing's sake. A point of controversy can be stated here. No dog can trail a wild creature in water or wet conditions. That is why a pack is used to flush out the quarry and is not trailing. Although otters are scarce in Staffordshire, in my poaching days I have seen them on three different streams — the Sow, the Meece and the river Tern; also once on the Gayton. In this one instance on the Gayton, two of us were out poaching and were about to cross a shallow ford. The otter was on the gravel on the opposite side and that was the last otter I have seen in my travels.

THE SCAVENGER FOX

There is not the same love for the foxes, and I have known quite a few people who would kill a fox without a second thought. On the other hand, I know farmers who will not allow the hunt on their lands on the grounds that foxes are scavengers and they clean up a lot of rubbish.

All the tales of the cleverness and craft of the fox is to me nothing but make believe to suit those who write stories of country life. These people build up some really fantastic and glamorous stories about foxes and what they will do. The fox is one of the dirtiest animals on our countryside. They will eat all kinds of carrion and country people will tell you that rotten fish will always attract them. I once heard this statement in a village inn during a talk about foxes. One man said, "Get some bad fish on a string and drag it across the fields where foxes are known to run. One could then lie in wait for the fox and shoot him."

This is not an experience of mine and so anyone can draw their own conclusions. If one knows where the council rubbish tips are in the country where holes are being filled in, foxes will often be seen at daybreak looking for food or hunting for rats. I have also seen foxes bolt out from ferrets. I also know several other people who claim to have had the same experience. One person claimed that he had caught five foxes out of a drain with ferrets on different visits. Some hunting people often talk a lot of drivel if they have a hound who tackles a fox single-handed. He is talked of as a great dog. It is a case of heavyweight against light-weight.

I have had cross-bred lurchers who would have killed any fox. They

39

talk of hounds following the scent of a fox. How can this be so when a pack of hounds are spread out over the fields. This cannot possibly be trailing a line of scent. To my way of reasoning it is like the otters, it is 'flushing out' and not trailing. Also on the day before the hunt meets men go out after dark and stop up the known fox earths. During the warm months, a fox earth will give off a bad smell due to the rotting of all kinds of rubbish. I have sometimes waited for foxes in the early hours of daybreak with a .22 rifle. For this kind of thing, one must have patience and understand the wind positions. It is no use waiting for foxes with the wind on your back.

Some people write some very queer stories about foxes, their hunting capabilities and their brains. I had more than one poacher friend who believed that a fox could not catch his own rabbits. To support their belief we have met foxes when we have been out in the night, and they have been travelling down wind. This is against all the rules of hunting. The point of this is that even poachers have to work into the wind. Sometimes we have met foxes and still we have caught rabbits off the same fields. I do not go along with these beliefs because foxes can catch rabbits where there is rough cover to allow them to get to close quarters. Here they can make a surprise rush at their quarry. There is one thing I hate about foxes. If they can find rabbits in snares, they will pull them to pieces and are not satisfied with a meal.

They do the same thing if they get in a poultry run. They kill the lot. As far as my own humble opinion goes, the fox to me is the English jackal. It is also surprising how near the towns foxes will make their homes. One very favourite place is the dirt mounds of coal mines. These are warm and dry.

CATS

On one estate some miles from the village where my old friends lived, they were engaged to do the trapping. A lot of trouble was being caused by prowling cats. The old rabbit trapper soon put paid to some of them because nothing on the countryside is as persistent or does more damage than a poaching cat. Some of these cats were caught in the traps in the burrows and these were promptly dispatched and buried out of sight. One trick I saw him carry out was as follows. He cut a hole in a dry plank sufficient to take a trap flat. This was placed over a small stream as a bridge. It was explained to me that cats do not like wet feet and they try to pick a dry path. These traps are not baited in any way but sometimes they can be successful. It is a nasty sight to watch a cat with a trapped or snared rabbit. They will straddle over the poor victim and slowly chew their ears off right down to the head while the victim is still alive. I have seen this on many occasions when trapping near farms. I have seen

Figure 2.9   The troublesome fox.

Figure 2.10   Poaching cats can also be very troublesome.

rabbits half eaten away by the process of cats, and the things cats will do to their victims has to be seen to be believed. Can anyone wonder why keepers and trappers alike simply loathe cats. A good cat skin is of good value in the fur market, but again this is a trade which is kept quiet because of sentimental people. Their value is over twenty times that of rabbit furs. I have often wondered if this is one of the reasons why so much cat stealing goes on in the cities and towns. The killing of cats even among gamekeepers and trappers has to be kept quiet. I have had cats in nets on occasions when we have been netting near farms and they can be very dangerous customers.

Poacher Allies

3

In the twilight hour, when the rear mouse is flitting,
  And from some gray ruin the owl's heard to shriek,
His low ruined hut oft is Hubert seen quitting,
  With net and with setter the meadows to seek;

Annals of Sporting

Figure 3.1   Pheasants, fair game for the poacher, but it is folly to steal geese or poultry.

POACHER ALLIES

Although I often worked alone, there were many occasions when I co-operated with other poachers. Some were true allies, but a few could not be trusted.

FOOLISH BEHAVIOUR

One night along with my trapper friends we were having a drink in a hotel in a market town about four miles from their village. There was another trapper in the bar room who had taken too much drink. He was talking 'out of school'. He had set so many snares and traps on an estate about two miles out of town. The next morning he found a note in a cleft stick thanking him for the information. Some of his rabbits had been taken due to him talking in the wrong place. The two culprits responsible for this theft were later caught at the same game and were heavily fined in the police court. Apparently, they had done the same thing to other men. The owner of that estate was the chief magistrate on the Justices Bench when I was in court for poaching on another big estate.

Another foolish trick was tried one night on a mill pond near the village where my friends lived. Here some of the geese used to sleep out and someone had a go at them. Two of them were shot. These two geese were later found abandoned in the fields. Those responsible were never found, and no-one found out the reason they were left after shooting them. These are the tricks, along with fowl stealing which are very often blamed on the poachers. It was a silly trick to do and a waste of time.

PROGRESSING ON

It was due to my trapper friends that I learned a great deal about those areas. I knew all the footpaths and shortcuts through the woods and the crossing points of streams. Both these characters are now beyond this life but I often recall the happy days I had in their company. Trapping, snaring, netting and gunning, it was all in their day's work. This type of man has forgotten more than a good many so-called nature writers will ever know about wildlife, and they were always happy. There were no worries of industrial life for them.

When they had passed on, I began to poach that countryside really hard. A team of three poachers was set up and a car was on the job. We had, of course, used cars before, but the majority of drivers soon give up. They do not like to take risks, and are not reliable. This particular driver was one of the best poachers' drivers I have ever had contact with. He was with us for a long time. He would take us anywhere we wished to go and I never knew him to be one minute out on time. He had a light fixed so that he could signal to us while he was a long way off to warn us that he was on the way. This signalling was used in the open country where there was a good view of the countryside.

The majority soon lose their nerve but not this one. He would go anywhere and now my knowledge of the countryside was invaluable. Regular work was scarce so we were not the only people on the poaching game, and there was sometimes trouble due to jealousy. I well remember one old hand at the game — a very rough, hard type of man who had been to prison for poaching. He was known among the poachers as the 'Black Fox' and a crafty old man he was too. He said I was only a pup at the game. One night we happened to be working in the same part of the country in the West of our county. We were doing well until we heard them at work beating to their nets. Instead of letting them know that we were there too, we kept quiet under cover. Only experienced poachers would understand what would happen in a case like this. They were too late. We had caught over a hundred rabbits but they had only a few. The 'Black Fox' and his friends were not the only ones who tried to upset us in the belief that they knew all the answers. No-one knows all the answers in this game.

Another poacher that I knew said that I only knew one part of the countryside. He was wrong. I could work for miles around in any direction. My boyhood wanderings had never been forgotten which was something they did not know. One night, two of us caught 112 rabbits. On the same series of woods on the same night, this man and two others had caught fourteen. When we met, they were actually coming down wind. He was a decent kind of man and I pointed out to him that he was working wrong. I have been out for very little gains at times, but it was not due to other poachers' superior knowledge.

These people began to realise that I was best left alone. A lot of my training had been in the heart of the countryside by real countrymen. The man I have mentioned above sometimes came to my home to tell me where he was going to work. I would then work somewhere else to

46

Figure 3.2 A country scene; successful poaching requires detailed knowledge of the
countryside.

give him a fair chance. I also gave him a few lessons on net-making.

In due time, the districts to the west of our county were getting thinned out of their game and needed a rest. One to two years' rest makes a great difference to wildlife. I began to take one or two of my poacher friends out to places they had never seen before. One of these men had been a sergeant in the army. He was the type of man who did not know the meaning of nerves. He had been a good boxer and he would stand up to anyone in either daylight or dark. He was a strong man and was always willing to carry the heaviest loads of game to the roadsides ready for the car. Double journeys meant nothing to him. He always said he was so pleased at being able to work with someone who knew how to poach. He was a hard character to be sure but he always played fair with me. We were good friends to the end of his days. If other men were talking about the poaching game, he would say, "I will back the curls against any of you any time you like."

We were out together one night on the estate of the Lord I have mentioned earlier, and we were surprised by two keepers. I was a bit suspicious that things were not quite right having had a blank set. I left him on the woodside to care for the nets while I did the beating. I saw him light up a cigarette and I knew that something had gone wrong. I went to meet him and he said quietly, "It's the keepers. I have told them to keep off while I have a smoke." This was his way of dealing with a situation and he kept close to me while I cleared up the nets. Again we had a blank. Those keepers did not tackle us and we got clear of the estate. It is not commonsense to stay anywhere when you have been disturbed because the game will not settle down again that night. We had already had two blank sets.

One night three of us had decided to have a go at an estate which was notoriously 'hot' and it had been given a long rest. This estate belonged to the 'County Sheriff' and was only about two miles from a police headquarters. It is curious to understand the clannish attachment between county police and this type of estate owner. Even the 'Black Fox' had been to prison for working on this estate. We had set the nets along a coach drive close to the hall and, while we were beating to the nets, someone was walking along the gravel drive. The next thing that happened was a fight with our ex-army friend, and there was a fair scuffle going on. I called to him to let the man go and, when he did so, the man ran for the hall as fast as he could. We had just time to clear up the nets and get out of the way when he came back with two more men and they had guns. They began to fire in the air and there was quite a bedlam of noise.

We were hiding in an osier bed between the drive and the river, and then the police patrol arrived on the scene. We heard the men say to the

Figure 3.3 Poachers watching, for both game and gamekeepers.

police, "It's poachers again, but they can't get away. The river is up."
That told us which way they expected us to go because we often crossed
the river at certain points. When things were quiet and the police had
moved off, we hid the nets and rabbits in the osiers. If we were caught,
we did not want to lose our nets. We went back into the woods and
worked our way off to the road, and we managed to get clear. Those nets
and the few rabbits were got back in a very cheeky way. The main drive
ran right through the estate. I went with a friend of mine in the car and
the nets and rabbits were picked up and we saw no-one. They would not
expect anyone to return in daylight.

WE SAVE A BOY

On one occasion, we were setting the nets on a big sandy warren on
the edge of a country lane in a valley to the west of our county. While the
nets were being set up, I heard a curious noise. I know most of the night
sounds but this was something new. I signalled a warning to my friends
that something was wrong. After a few minutes of quiet listening, the
sounds were heard again. Two of us went up that hedge cover carefully,
and I had a flashlight ready in my hand. The cause of those sounds was
found. It was a little boy about six years old curled up in the hedge
bottom and very frightened. When we had calmed him down, he told us
that he was lost. He was nearly twenty miles from home. Our ex-army
friend stayed with the boy and kept him warm while two of us carried on
work. When the car picked us up in the morning, we took the boy with
us. Our brains must have been fuddled, or we were thinking of the boy's
safety and nothing else. Getting near home, we drove straight to the
police station and I went in to hand the boy over. I told the policeman in
charge what had happened. I was, of course, in my rough poaching
clothes but he did not say anything, only to thank me for looking after
the boy. On the way out, I met a policeman coming in for his day shift
duty. He was a neighbour of mine and he knew me well.

"Where have you been?" he bawled at me. "Not picking mushrooms," I answered back. Before he recovered from the answer, I was in
the car and away for home. We did not hear anything from the police
but later a letter was received from the boy's parents thanking us for the
trouble we had taken. The reason we did not take the boy to his own
home direct was that he lived at the opposite end to us and the police and
their courts in that area were a bit savage against poachers. It was a case
of "All's well that ends well".

A NARROW ESCAPE

Another exciting incident along with my ex-army friend and another poacher happened on a well-keepered estate on the east side of our county. There had been some trouble with a contraption known as **trip wire alarm guns**. These were rigged up by the keepers on fence posts in the woodsides. I had done some very careful scouting on that estate and sometimes I knew where those alarm guns might be set. In order to defeat their object, I used to go along the covers or woodsides slowly with a long stick held out in front of me. The nets were set following me along very carefully. If I came to a trip wire, I warned my friends and held the wire in my hands while the nets were passed over or under it. On this particular night, we had worked two woods and had no trouble. On the third wood, a long fir plantation holding a lot of pheasants, and the keeper's house at the far end, our poacher friend insisted on taking first lead with the nets. He was one of that type who think they know it all. Thirty yards out and 'Bang', he had hit the wire. In the confusion that followed he spun round and caught himself fast by his feet in his own net.

The keepers were out in a few seconds and our man was in trouble. We had to drag him to cover and cut that net. Before we got clear, the police patrol arrived on the scene, and we were in the wood. It was a good thing

Figure 3.4 The keeper's house lay at the far end of the wood.

51

that I knew that country very well. We had to make a long detour across country to get away. All the rabbits we had caught off the first two woods, and the net which we cut were lost. There was almost a fight between us over this affair. It was a night out for nothing but that poacher never tackled that estate again.

It was a curious happening that, about two years after this skirmish, I was in an hotel along with my wife and the man at the next table was talking to me. I know you, he said, "I am the keeper of .... estate. It was you who was involved in some of the poaching on my place." There was a good laugh when he described some of the incidents. He told me that I had been noticed when looking round in the daytime. The family who owned that estate have practically died out and, during their last years, the great hall has been pulled down and sold. This lovely estate was broken up and sold to land-grabbing speculators. Now a lot of it has houses built on it.

One night, four of us were going out to a big estate in the west of our county and we were travelling by train. We had arranged for the car to pick us up in the morning to save the driver a double journey. The idea was to work in two pairs in different parts. Who should get into the same carriage as us but a retired police sergeant and he knew us. He was living on a farm in that area. After this accidental meeting, further poaching in that area had to have a rest due to the keepers and farmers being warned. It is surprising what they will do to stop the poachers — such things as putting loose thorns, cut thistles, and rusty old barbed wire on the woodsides to foul up the nets.

MEETING 'OLD JOHN'

Sometime in the late 'twenties, I got to know an old man living in the west of our county, right on the Shropshire border. I was invited over to his cottage and this was to be the cause of meeting one of the best poachers who lived in this country. There was almost an instant friendship between us. He would often sit and tell me stories of poaching escapades in his younger days in various parts of the country. The old poacher stood over six feet and was slimly built. A grey billy goat beard reached down his chest, a sharp nose, and keen black eyes. He was something similar to my old friend 'Moley Jack'. In his working life, he had been a timber feller in the woods all over the country. He had been a poacher all his life and he knew the ways of the woodland wild-life. Birds and wild animals were like a book to him and what he did not know about them was not worth bothering about. He was to be my teacher for the next year or two and even when he was too old for the poaching game, he would take me walking and show me different places in that area. He was not caught often in over fifty years of poaching and one of these arrests was in my company. When we were finally caught, the police sergeant who carried out the arrest told me that old John was the cleverest poacher he had ever known. When the police came to interview me at home he advised my wife to keep me at home away from him. The police do not have to encourage law breakers. I remained friends with John to the end of his days. The tricks that we got up to would fill a book. He had two nephews who were gamekeepers on an estate and even these were not left alone. It was these keepers who eventually had us arrested, but they did not do it themselves, they called in the police.

What caused us to be arrested was not actually our poaching. It was the result of several small happenings and our sublime cheek. One mistake that was made was in using the village inn too often. John's cottage was next to the inn. This is something that can be dangerous. A village inn properly used is a gold mine for country information but in one's rough clothes for night poaching and in the company of a character like him it was simply inviting trouble. A certain dealer used to go round that countryside buying up poultry, rabbits or what he could get, and he always called at John's cottage. I could get a far better price for ours in the town and this led to grumbling from him. In fact one business man in town used to pay me six pence per head more for netted rabbits. He always said to me that they were for his best customers.

Another slight mistake was when we were using the car. There was a garden track to John's cottage and the car stopping here in the early hours would soon be noted. He taught me how to study the lie of the land while sitting quietly on a vantage point. To take note of the twists and bends of the woods and how various winds would affect each side of a wood. I knew a lot about this subject but extra teaching hurts no one. He taught me how to set a hedgerow twice if the wind was on the 'Shoulder' or 'End on', and the correct times and way to net open warrens. Also to study the contours of hills and valleys, and how the wind would pull into valleys and be in a different direction to the wind on higher ground. He taught me the secrets of the 'bont line' which can only be used on clean and fairly flat fields. Incidentally we had been using the 'bont line' when we were arrested.

It was with John that I first saw a ride net used at night-time. Living in the country he could pick the spots for these nets. He used ride nets only on dark nights, and he used a light on the net. I think that man could catch anything, but these nets are not a paying proposition, and also it is not a method I care for. For one thing too many small birds are caught and these have to be got out and set free as I have stated before.

When we were not busy on the poaching he would sit and tell me stories of poaching incidents in his younger days. He described to me a

Figure 3.5 Battle between poachers and gamekeepers

pitched battle between gamekeepers and poachers after pheasant poaching on an estate in Lancashire. One keeper and two poachers were injured in the fight. The two who were injured were sentenced to five years in prison and the other two got away. John was not concerned in this affair. He was working on timber felling in that area.

One story John told me was about a poacher friend of his from the next village. He had what is known as a double meshed net and I know that these are good because I have made and used them. They are made by knitting two strands of high quality fine hemp when making the net. This man was caught and prosecuted in a nearby market town. The policeman who caught him, while giving his evidence in court said, "Your honour, he is not satisfied with one net he has to have two fastened together."

He told me about the Norfolk poacher, about whom Lilias Rider Haggard wrote a book entitled, *I walked by Night. The King of the Norfolk Poachers.* He had met him in Lancashire while they were engaged on timber felling on one of the big estates. They got together and were poaching the hares and other game off that and other estates. John told me how a market was found for the game. Hares in those days were 'hot game'. John went in to town and walked into the biggest game shop he could find and asked for the owner. He asked the owner if he would care to buy some hares. The owner of that shop looked at John and probably noted that he was a countryman, and invited him into his office. A deal was made as soon as the man knew it was poached game. It was also arranged that the game would be picked up by pony and trap while he was on his rounds.

He proved a good man to those poachers while they worked in Lancashire. John told me it was always cash down and a good price. The owner of that estate was one of the leading men in this country in the sporting world so I do not wish to state his name. If my memory is to be trusted I think John told me that the name of the Norfolk man was Rawson or Rawley, but I am not sure. He came from near Bungay. He had been to prison in Norwich a few times for poaching. He also told me that this man ended his own life by hanging in a barn when he was eighty years old. It was from the scrap books he left behind that Lilias Rider Haggard wrote the book. Life must have been really hard in those days.

*Published by Boydell

Figure 4. Collecting the Hare

Places and More Adventures

4

Figure 4.1 Waterfowl; such fowl often supplemented the meagre fare during the days of
starvation pay.

PLACES AND MORE ADVENTURES

I have tried to keep names out of these memoirs, but I do not think it will cause any embarrassment to anyone if I mention some of the places where we carried out our poaching escapades. My poaching days are long since over. The countryside about John's cottage was worked very heavy during the time I was working with him. There was very little work to be had in those days and it was starvation pay. Still people have to have food. For myself I did not intend to go short of food or other needs if I could prevent it. One night on a place some miles from John's cottage by using the 'bont lines' three of us caught just under two hundred rabbits. This catch was picked up and taken to a dealer in town. The same dealer who I have mentioned for paying me extra. We worked all around the Broughtons, Hales, Bishops Woods, Burnt Woods, Winnington, Old Springs, Oakley, and other places such as Redcastle and Hawkestone in Shropshire.

On one of these places close to John's cottage there were a few hares. He had been asked to get one or two. He took me out one night to this place and he set two hare nets about 100 yards apart in a country lane. We then beat up a big meadow land towards the nets and that set caught three nice hares. He explained to me that this was only one of the ways to catch them and that hares like to run on a dry lane. These were left behind while we carried out further netting for the rabbits. In nine cases out of ten when hares are running in daytime they stop and take a look round before passing through a hedge. This only applies when they are not disturbed. If snares are set on a hedge run benders should be used over the snare to make the hare keep low when going through. These benders which of course are twigs, prevent the hare from hitting the top wire of the snare. This method of using benders over the snares will catch other wildlife from pheasants to foxes.

Steel traps are also deadly in the same position. It is against the law to

59

Figure 4.2 Pheasants provide the night sport known as 'jerking'.

use steel traps in hedge bottoms.* Another law which cannot be watched, but poachers, game keepers, and others will break all these laws.

One moonlight night he asked me if I would like a night out 'Jerking'. This was his own expression by which he meant pheasants and out we went with a gun. He took me down the sides of the woods and through the rides facing the wind in much the same way as poaching the rabbits. He told me to look carefully into the trees, looking up into the light of the sky. When he first fired the noise to me seemed to be terrific. I said to him that everyone on the countryside would know that someone was poaching. His answer to me was, "We are quite safe, if anybody knows that we are gunning they will stay in bed." Working on this principle I have seen him shoot pheasants only a few yards away from a country house.

NIGHT GUNS

Night gunning is real good poaching sport, but the penalties behind it are very heavy. This kind of poaching comes under "Criminal Law", and not only the poaching Acts. The "Four Ten" is a good type of gun for this kind of work especially if used along with luminous sights. This kind of poaching is best carried out in the late months of the year when the trees are bare. One place we went to for pheasants was facing a main road and when I pointed out to John that the country house was at the bottom of the big wood he said, "Yes, I know, but they will be wondering if it is a gun or motor back fires they can hear. We shall be able to get a couple of shots in before we move on." This to me was really cheeky. He told me that if a man uses a gun when it is going dusk it is very difficult to judge the direction of the sound and this enables the poacher to get away. This shooting at dusk was done mainly by pothunters to supply their own table.

The roosting places of pheasants are varied. A thorn scrub is a good place to find them. If a good patch of thorn trees can be found either in a wood or nearby the pheasants will roost there. Between the boughs of such trees as the oaks is another good place because they can sit flat. They also like thick old ivy. It is very difficult to find them when they roost in the big firs in hard weather. Pheasants will be seen to gather together in numbers under the oak trees when acorns are ripe and where sugar beet is piled. These could be deadly places to use traps. At night-time the strength of the wind must be taken notice of, because wind will affect the height at which the birds will roost.

*Many traps such as the notorious gin trap are now illegal and the gamekeeper is advised to study a modern book such as *Ratting and Rabbiting* by Guy N. Smith, published by Saiga Publishing Co.Ltd.

61

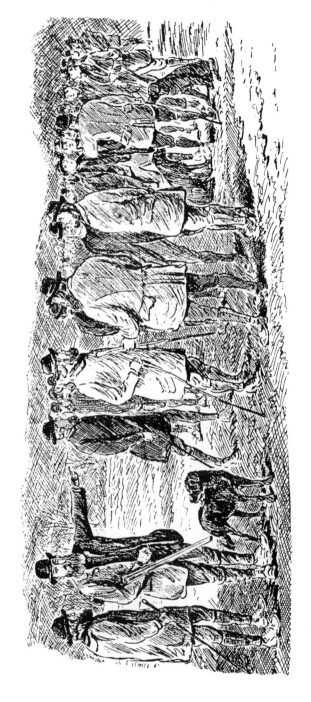

Figure 4.3 Gentry tend to spin yarns about their shooting experiences, seen here with beaters and gamekeepers assembled for a pheasant shoot.

One of the things that I do not agree with is those shooting people who always try to make others believe that their quarry has almost human intelligence. Some writers too are guilty of this. This is an example. Some years after John died I was in a country inn along with some friends of mine. We were listening to the general gossip and a party of the so called "Gentry" were talking of the pheasant shooting. One man was telling his friends a story of a cock pheasant a few days back when the shoot was on. This wily bird had stayed under a thick blackberry bush and let the beaters pass by. His statement was that he had one of the beaters going back into the spinney to find the bird. To get him to move the beater had to push the bird out to provide his master with a shot. He did not say who had seen the bird in the first place because the gunners are outside the woods.

These people were also talking of winter holidays in the sun so I do not think my poaching days will ever hurt my conscience. As we were leaving the inn, I said "Sir, next time you go pheasant shooting shake a box of matches and you may do better."

CAUGHT BY A TRIP WIRE

Back to my days with John. One night John and myself were netting rabbits in the Winnington district and while I was working up a cover side towards Lordsley I struck a trip wire. Talk about night-time shocks. I thought we had been shot at. My old friend was furious about this. "I know who has done this. I'll steady him the old so and so. He's let the shooting and he thinks he will stop us from catching anything." He was quite wild about these trip wires because when they go off it upsets everything for that night. When we got home he said "I'll have some of those rabbits despite what he does." For a long time after that night that particular wood was always referred to as the "Gun wood". It was actually Little Manchester woods.

During the following week John set up a team of four poachers and this was to be my first meeting with two brothers from the Shropshire district. They were sons of one of his bygone friends and good poachers they were too. They worked a slightly different method than we did. Instead of using big pockets for their nets they had a bag much like a newsboy. This was fastened to a waist belt to prevent it from slipping round the shoulders. They had good long nets up to ninety yards long. Just think what four nets like these can do in the hands of good men who know what they are doing. Incidentally those trip wire guns were only set on one wood.

These two brothers had market stalls and also had their own car, and this is where the rabbits went to. We never knew if the man who had set those trip wires ever realised what was done to his rabbits. We hit that place very hard until John called a halt. On one set in a valley near Winnington we killed 112 rabbits in one hit by using the 'bont lines'. These two brothers were later to take me into some of the Shropshire districts although I knew a lot of places in Shropshire. They too knew their way about the country. The man who had set those alarm guns was classed in that countryside as a dangerous madman, but he did not frighten everyone as he thought. We often wondered how mad he would have been if he had known how close to his farm we sometimes set the nets. Still, later on two poachers were caught on these grounds and they lost all their nets as well as a prosecution.

The Haunted Wood

One day I was in the countryside and somewhere between the Oakley Folly woods and the Daisy lakes I came across a nice lot of rabbits and it looked to me that no one was troubling them. I asked John what was wrong with this place because even he had given it a miss for a long time and yet it was not far from his home. He told me a nice little story that had somehow got around. It was supposed to be haunted. I never did believe in these yarns about ghosts and spirits so I begged him to have a go at them. He agreed to this but he insisted on one net and his gun and he was to stay with the net. We were going very well off that place until we saw that ghost. I was well away from the woodside and I could see a pale blue light wavering down by the wood. It looked a little bit uncanny but John had his gun ready and soon put paid to that ghost. It turned out to be an owl and somehow it had got some white phosphorus stuff on its wings and body. Probably from roosting inside dead old trees. That was the end of the Folly ghost. I have seen the same kind of thing since that affair on other owls. I have also seen it on badgers. There was once a ghost scare in the Chetwynd Park area near Newport until someone decided to shoot and this turned out to be a badger walking on the roads. People who believed in spirits were trying to play up this ghost affair at Newport, and also at Little Weston near Stafford. At various times I have poached all around Newport, but I was not troubled by any ghosts.

FISHING FOR A CHANGE

In the spring months the old fellow used to go after the fish in the stream which feeds Bearstone Mill near Winnington. This stream is the River Tern which starts its course at Maer Hall. Netting fish is a good sport but in streams like this the money gain is very little. Still poaching is poaching and the thrill of the game is like a fever once you get in it, and John believed in harvesting what he could off the countryside. To tell of one instance of John's clever tricks this is what I actually saw done in

Figure 4.4 The owl and the haunted wood.

broad daylight. I had gone over to see him for some reason not to do with poaching. Along with others he was working in the corn fields harvest-ing. I went up to the fields to see him and he told me that bailiffs and keepers were working too. He confided to me to go and get a rabbit net and pegs and to be careful. I did so and I kept out of sight of the other harvesters. At dinner time everybody except John and another man went down to the village inn. When all was quiet that net was quickly set up the hedge side and these two men walked through what little corn was still standing and beat up slowly towards the net. While I watched some young pheasants walked out towards the net. There was a sudden rush at the birds and before some of them could rise they were in that net. They were bundled up and the birds and net were put in a sack. I took them to John's cottage but believe me, I was more at ease once I had got them home. If I had met any of those farmers or keepers they may have guessed that something was wrong. These are poachers' tricks and are not the methods of general poaching. It was as John said later, "Those keepers should have given a little more thought to those young birds." They were still in their first brown feathers. It is not very often that keepers make these mistakes.

65

THE AIRSHIP DISASTER

One Saturday night on the Broughton's estate we were at work and in this particular instance we had set the nets on a corn stubble. There was a good wind and the sort of night when the clouds were moving fast. While we were on this field there was a great flash of light across the sky and the rabbits could be seen running towards the nets. The light died away slowly and at first we thought it was lightning, but we could not understand why there was only one flash and no thunder. The time of the flash was 2.10 a.m. the fourth of October, 1930. The next morning when I got home I heard the news of the R101 airship disaster at Beauvais in France. I did not think of any connection with this disaster until later. A lady who had got out of bed at her home in Market Drayton to close the windows saw that flash of light and she noted the time as 2.10 a.m. She wrote a letter to the *Evening Sentinel* to ask if anyone else had seen that flash. I did not answer it for obvious reasons, but it seemed quite a coincidence. This would prove to anyone how far light from an explosion like this will travel. This disaster was over four hundred miles away. To anyone who does not believe what I have just written above these statements could be verified by writing to the *Evening Sentinel*.

THE POACHERS TRAPPED

It was later in the same year that John and I were caught. The keepers must have guessed that we were poaching on the Broughton and Fair Oak districts. One of them had the notion of tying a single strand of black cotton to some of the small gates on the estates. These small gates were for the use of the fox hunting people. We called them the hunting wickets. Eventually one Thursday night we broke some of these strands and they knew that we were on the estate. The police were called in and along with the keepers they waited for us in the garden of John's cottage. We were cornered without much chance and a scrap started up. When the police sergeant blew his whistle we knew then who they were. Although John was getting on in years he was kept between two police-men because they seemed to think he might strike out at the keepers. They told him not to start any further trouble to make matters worse. I was taken to the village inn which was the nearest place with a phone. My own local police were informed and my name was verified as correct. The police took our nets and thirty-six rabbits as evidence against us. They also took our bont line reel.

When the upset had quietened down and all details were taken, I passed a remark to the police sergeant and said, "I am glad you did not catch us the last time we were out." "Why?" he asked. I told him that if he had there would have been a far better haul of rabbits for him. A few days later I was interviewed at home by the country police. When they came to my home they had with them a local policeman and my father. This policeman was rather bombastic the way he talked to me. He wanted to know all my friends in the game and all the places I had been to. He wanted to know everything. I am no squealer and I told him he was not clever enough to trace a bad smell in a fish market and to get out, the job was nothing to do with him. When he walked out the sergeant who had caught us was grinning and said, I was in order because they held the warrant.

Incidentally, it was the same policeman that I met on the morning that the little boy was handed over. When all the details had been dealt with they even asked my wife what I did with the money I earned from poaching. Believe me these things count a lot when you end up in court. Those country police were good sports and they took my father for a few drinks without asking any more questions. A few weeks later we were prosecuted at Eccleshall before Major Moate of Horsley Hall. The summons was very quaintly worded and apart from poaching we were charged with using engines for the taking and killing of game. This was referring to our 'bont line' reel. I shall never forget the day that our case was tried. It caused quite a laugh. The police sergeant was talking to John and myself quite friendly and he told us the keepers were there to give evidence against us. He asked me how much we sold our rabbits for and when I told him he laughed and said, "I have not done badly then. I have had more for them than you, but the money goes to charity." "Who cares," I said, "It will do someone some good."

Our names were called out for trial. We stood there facing the 'Bench', John in his rough country cords and his long beard, and I was in a light grey suit and smartly dressed. Major Moate the chief magistrate had rimless glasses right on the end of his nose, and a shiny bald head. I do not know how I kept my face straight. The charges were called out to us. "You are charged with poaching at night-time with long nets and engines, and the taking of game." We pleaded guilty.

The chief Magistrate had a long look at us over his glasses. It seemed comical to me that his eyes appeared to be above his glasses. He said, "My word, we have the old fox and his cub." The policeman who was in the witness box giving evidence said, "Your honour, he is no cub. He is as bad as the old fox for poaching," and he held up for inspection by the Bench a new light brown net 90 yards (27.43 m) long, and it was a high quality net, the first and only time it had ever been used. Major Moate asked us about the thrills of night poaching and how we worked. He was told that even his estate was not safe. He just smiled when I said that I knew my way about his estate. I had worked on it with my bygone

Figure 4.5 Local police examining a poacher's haul; there were good and bad sorts among them.

trapper friends. After a few questions to the police we were fined only lightly and I nearly threw my hat in the air. Major Moate had proved out what we had been told, that he was a very decent man and was highly respected in those districts.

After the case was over we adjourned to the Crown Hotel and the police concerned in the case came in and had drinks with us. There were never any ill feelings between us. It was as the sergeant said, it was their job when called out to deal with any law breaking. I carried the name of John's cub for a time after this affair. The fines were paid one Saturday morning and when I had been given the receipt for them I put two rabbits on the desk out of a bag I had with me. That policeman's eyes popped. "You cheeky devil, but thanks, and good luck to you."

I knew a few poachers who always said that new nets were cursed with bad luck. I do not believe in superstitition; to me it is nothing but fear and a weak mind. To show one cause of men poaching in those years was the fact that my own earnings were twenty six shillings for three days working naked on a hot coal face.

There was a sad ending to one of the policemen who came to my home. The one in the witness box as I have stated before. In later years he was made a sergeant in the Flintshire force. The tragedy was that he lost both his legs through illness. In 1973 there was an article in the *Evening Sentinel* from the Chief Constable of the Flintshire force. This sergeant was being presented with a greenhouse from his friends. Someone had written a letter to him about our arrest and other incidents in country life, and asking him if he remembered those days. The Flintshire Chief said the letter had greatly cheered the unfortunate man. He stated in his article to the *Evening Sentinel* that he remembered his country days and that I was the youngest among the known poachers. His name was Constable G. Bowers.

FURTHER PROSECUTIONS

Within a few weeks of our court case three other poachers were caught and were prosecuted in another county town court. This particular court had a reputation of severity against any petty law breakers. They were caught when they were leaving the estate I have written about as 'hot' on an earlier page. These three were fined over ten times as much as we were fined for the same kind of law breaking. In later years two out of the same three were caught at Fradswell and they were fined too heavily in any decent man's mind for an offence like poaching. They were fined a total of £50 each and costs. This was the heaviest fine ever inflicted for this kind of offence in the whole of the Midlands in those years, and this was in the same court.

This is another example of the same court and nothing to do with poachers. Two men were using ferrets and guns with the permission of the farmer. One of them only winged a rabbit which managed to run a short distance on to the next farm. He fetched this rabbit and was fined £25 for trespassing, in pursuit of game. One of the men who paid the £50 wrote to lawyers about the heavy fines, but he did not get any satisfactory answers. I have my own opinions about lawyers and some magistrates. These vicious fines were nearly all inflicted by people who hid their true character under the cloak of religion. It has happened in other courts.

TROUBLE WITH THE CLERGY

I carried on poaching along with John for sometime after being in court. Only a few weeks after being caught we were using a bont line at Fair Oak near the Broughtons and someone was on the same field. They cut that line but no one came near us. We always thought it was the keeper. John taught me my way about these areas for miles around, and the knowledge came in useful long after his death.

I would like to show up the hypocrisy under which some people try to live. The village vicar from close to where my friend lived tried to get John and his wife moved out of their cottage on account of our poaching. This hypocrite may never have known if we had not been caught. Like a good many more people he was fussing around the estate owners, and wealthy farmers. He did not succeed because poacher or not, the village people liked the old couple. That vicar would have seen them homeless, possibly to end their days in the workhouse, and they were then about seventy-three years old.

Long after John's death I met this vicar quite by accident in my parent's home. He was paying a visit to an aunt of mine and she was taking him around to visit her relatives. It was sheer coincidence that I should happen to call on my parents at the same time. When I learned who the man was I must have seen red. I reminded him of old John and told him who I was. I asked him if remembered John's wife, Emma, saying to him "Mind your own affairs. The Lord did not provide food for the rich alone. Do you, you hypocrite think so?' That vicar and my aunt had the best tongue lashing they had ever had. They did not stay for tea because I told the pair of them to clear out at once. My aunt did not object to poached game if she could have it cheap. My mother was quite upset over this and said that I ought to be ashamed of myself, but why should I? John was a far better man than all his kind. The cottage where my friend lives was allowed to go to ruin, but I often think of the happy times I had there with one of the best poachers I ever knew. Where his cottage stood and the garden are now a car park for a village inn.

70

FURTHER ADVENTURES

I sometimes met that police sergeant in later times and he was always the 'Gentleman'. Once I met him in a hotel. I had been out in the countryside for the day along with my wife, and while we were talking over a drink I told him of a big park I had visited that day in Shropshire. He said, "Wouldn't you like to get at that place."

"Don't worry yourself," I answered him. "I'll hit that place when I want to." He advised my wife to keep me at home. That police sergeant eventually rose to be an Inspector in one of the industrial town of South Staffordshire.

On one occasion some years after these happenings I took a friend of mine on a poaching trip on an estate close to Bridgenorth. We decided to travel home via Wolverhampton. I told my friend that if we did get stopped on the way there would be quite a laugh if the Inspector was still there. My friend was a novice just learning about the game and he was surprised that I was known for poaching so far from home. He had a bigger shock when I told him that I was known in various parts of the country including the Isle of Man.

Regarding the court I have mentioned for its severity there was one case in which I was slightly concerned. Two of us had brought a nice lot of rabbits to the roadside ready to be picked up in the morning. My friend was crossing the road ready to work another part and had not noticed three people coming along the road. He was too late to move to cover before being seen. He must have thought that everyone who is about at night-time are all poachers. The three were a policeman and a farmer and his wife. They had been to a late dance and were upset because two tramps were asleep on their drive. Knowing that the policeman was close to they had fetched him to the scene. My friend was the first one they came to and he was arrested. The policeman had spotted a bag in the hedge as he searched around. Along with some of the rabbits he was taken to the police station while I was still behind the hedge with the rest. When the notice of prosecution was delivered a week later the prosecution was in the name of the farmer. I knew at once what their move was. If that farmer gave evidence in court he would claim for loss of time and money, and possibly the money for the rabbits and net. The point was that the arrest was on the 'King's Highway', a public road, and not on private land. We went to see the police Superintendent and told him the prosecution was wrong. It should have been a police prosecution and not in the name of the farmer. He wanted the notice back to issue another one, but we refused.

When the case came up for trial the farmer was not even called to give evidence and we got away with a few shillings costs and the net was returned. We did not trouble about the rabbits because we

71

suspected that they would be shared up among the police. After this the police had that man in court on three occasions and he got a heavy fine each time. The first time he was caught after paying costs of court there were also two other men caught with him. He was fined twice as much as the other two so it is obvious this was to level up the first case. They never did manage to get me in that court. My poaching days are over but I do know they would have put a very heavy fine on me.

THE DANGERS OF AMATEURS

After John's passing I worked for a while with one or two local men but in my opinion they were not good poachers. They were men who did not study things for themselves and they had to trust to other people's knowledge. They worked with such men as the "Black Fox" who I mentioned earlier and one or two others who knew something about the game. The money they used to get was spent mostly in the local bars and their poaching places were soon known to all. I soon left these men alone. I decided about this time to go out farther afield and change country.

JONATHAN — A FRIEND FOR LIFE

I teamed up with another good poacher. His name was Jonathan and he was a real good man on the job. We worked together for some years and we remained good friends right to the end of his days. When our poaching days were over we often used to yarn about our experiences and the things we had done. He was an expert at snaring and he loved his snares as much as I loved my nets. We have had some wonderful and exciting times together, and sometimes dangerous moments. We were

Figure 4.6 Jonathon's brother had a small farm we sometimes worked from.

game enough to tackle any estate and with my own knowledge of the countryside we could work anywhere from Derbyshire to Shropshire to South Staffs.

At one time he had a brother living well in the countryside and we sometimes worked from his small farm. One night we had set two nets along a big wood on some high ground overlooking a big lake and Hall. A lovely place in the daytime. In the field were some pig arks and while we were beating down to the nets I tapped one of these arks with my stick. The door flew open and a voice said, "It's about time you had come. I've been here two hours with this sow." I did not answer and crept away quietly back to the nets. I wondered what went through that fellow's mind when he found there was no-one there. Possibly he things were a little spooky. These are the sudden surprises that can trip up the poacher.

In the company of Jonathan we poached all over the country from the Weaver Hills to the heart of Shropshire and out beyond the Bromleys. He was the type of man who did not panic or lose his nerve and like myself he loved to fetch the game from places which were thought to be 'hot'. He would poach as much for devilment as for money. He told me once about a lucky escape he had when he was out with a lurcher bitch he owned. They were in some bushes and the dog slipped into a fairly deep hole. He went straight to the nearest farm for a rope and got the lurcher out. It was lucky that he did not fall in as well.

During the war he actually did a trout poaching job in Italy. He wrote a letter to me to tell me all about it. We were out together one Christmas Eve and I told him that I had seen hares running along a gritty road leading to the Hall. We had set the nets on two small spinneys and we took care to cross the road putting pegs on each side on the grass verges. It paid off alright and besides the rabbits we got two hares, but while we were busy a pony and trap came along the road. I called to Jonathan, "Take the pegs out quick." This was to allow the pony to go through while the net was flat. Instead of doing this he stood in the front of his net and stopped that pony. "Hold it a minute," he said and two farmers who had been drinking got out of the trap. "What's the matter?" they asked. Jonathan calmly explained that we had nets set across the road. Those farmers went off the beam end alright. They were fussing and cursing us. They were yelling at us and calling us thieves. Jonathan asked them to be quiet. 'Why don't you belt up. How can we catch anything if you are bawling about the place?" He was a big fellow and could well hold his own in a scrap.

THE CHALLENGE

One farmer, who we knew, had put wire netting fences round three small separate sandy warrens. They were like three circles in the field on some rising ground. The man was a greyhound owner and breeder and was a member of a racing combine. These rabbits were used to train their dogs before they went on the raching tracks. They would not have interested us only for what he said to Jonathan. He said that no-one would take his few rabbits. Not even us two and he happened to know us. In the early spring Jonathan and myself went to that place in the moonlight with wire cutters. We cut bob holes in the bottoms of the fences. It was good meadowland. The bob holes were never noticed as the meadow grass grew and the rabbits were using them well. As soon as the fields outside the fences were cut and the late hay moved off we set into those rabbits. When rabbits are left alone for a full breeding season like this they soon multiply, and it was surprising what we caught. It was as Jonathan remarked, "He should not have said anything to me. Then he would have been left alone." This was a typical example of what Jonathan would do. We did not trouble that man again after we had taken off a good number of his rabbits.

THE BULLYING FARMER

There was one place in particular which we poached very heavily. We hit this place with everything. Nets, snares, and guns. This was all because we were threatened with violence. The man who caused the trouble owned a very extensive farm. It was a big area some of which was wild land plus the woodlands. He had a family of hefty looking sons, but they were nothing but a brutal cowardly lot. There were a few court cases over these sons knocking people about, but they always brawled when they were two or three to one. One of these sons made a very bad mistake one night. He tangled with the ex-army sergeant I mentioned earlier. This was nothing to do with me, but I was told that he got laid out cold.

Jonathan and myself set about that place for all we could get. Rabbits, hares, a few wild ducks, and an odd pheasant or two were taken. Unknown to this farmer Jonathan had obtained the trapping rights on another farm close by. I also had farmer friends where we could leave the motor. This farmer knew what we were doing and he kept quiet. I have not seen this place for some years, but I do not think it ever recovered from our attentions. It was nets, snares, traps, and guns at every chance we had. The hares on the place used to harbour up in some old beds of dry rushes. They did not last long, Jonathan was a good man with his snares. On this area were a few small ponds where wild ducks used to

Figure 4.7   Hares provide good sport.

75

feed. Sometimes on moonlight nights we have crept up to these ponds with a twelve bore gun. Shoot, pick up, and move away back into the woods was our method.

One night I was in a country inn close to these areas and I was in the company of some country men who I knew. The man who had been threatening us came in. After a while he could not rest and the subject of the poachers came up. He said what he would do if he caught anyone and looked at me. "That's a big if," I said in reply. The local policeman came in with his wife and this farmer was trying to make a fuss of him probably on account of the troubles his sons had been involved in.

"You can come for a bit of shooting any time you like Mr . . . " "There's a few hares on the Well meadow now." I looked at him and said, "Mr . . . he is too late to shoot them. They have found a new home." My farmer friends said that I should not have told him. Probably the drink had made me careless, but to my way of thinking it sometimes does good to give an answer like that to his kind of people. I do not like threats of violence and he was told that if ever his sons attacked me retaliation would certainly follow. After we had cleared what we could off this place we began to go out to the Kings Bromley, Bagots Park and Abbotts Bromley areas. This was really good country in the years long before the war and along with Jonathan we had some tremendous hauls off these areas.

Playing Toreador

It was here at what we called the "Five mile point" that we once played the part of "Toreador." It was all very well to smile about it later but it was no laughing matter then. This bull was under an oak tree standing out from the woodside. The nets were to go between the tree and the woodside. There were a few cows under the tree and among them was this bull, and he bowled Jonathan over before we knew what was happening. I always carried with me a powerful torch and if anyone who ever reads this fancies a bit of poaching make a powerful torch a necessity. I flashed the light on that bull and the temporary blindness gave my friend a chance to get into the wood. I backed away while switching the light on and off. I had to do this in order to get where the woodside fence would let me through without any delay. I charged for that cover and made it safely. My friend came to me and we lay very quiet listening for that bull. He was snorting up and down that fence and eventually he began to tear up the nets. We were on that field for more than two hours before we could make any move to get the nets away. Even then one was absolutely ruined. That was one night when things went badly wrong. Jonathan said, "Lady Luck" had deserted us, but we had no personal injuries.

Figure 4.8 Playing the part of Toreador to an angry bull like this was no laughing matter.

TROUT MAKE A PLEASANT CHANGE

One place we used to visit very often was the valley at Abbotts Bromley where the new Blithfield reservoirs were built. In the middle of the valley was an old mill on the river Blythe. There was a long mill pond, and a sluice by the side of the mill to take away the overflow water. In the sluice the water was no more than two feet deep and was always choked full of fish, a lot of them good big trout. Just try to imagine what this meant. Two brick walls, a concrete bottom and only one way out. A 3 yard (2.7 m) trammel net would have caught all those fish, and another point is that other fish would have taken their place from the two streams; the Blythe and the Tad. Those trout can thank their lucky stars that we were more interested in other game. There was not much money to be earned in poaching fresh water fish. That mill is now under water so no one can take any advantage of what I have written. I have often thought of the times that we have gazed at those fish on moonlight nights and talked of what could be done with them. Still these are nice memories and I would like to fish those reservoirs in lawful methods.

My friend once taught me a trick of trout poaching in broad daylight. I know some tricks but this was one of the best I have ever seen. He asked me to make a trammel net. When it was made I went with him on this trout excursion, one day in June. It was a lovely sunny day. I openly chided him and said he was scatter brained, but was he. I was due to be taught different. On getting to the appointed spot he stripped off naked and got in the stream. I was amazed at this action when he stretched the net out and began to go up that stream. Away up that stream was a culvert which ran under the railway lines. As he slowly approached the dark tunnel there was not a fish to be seen. He entered that tunnel backwards with the net outstretched in his hands. In a few minutes he was out again with enough fish to fill a bucket. As he dressed I sat down and tried to reason this one out. Groping, when the water is low, night lines with worms, the uses of chemicals, and explosives. I knew about these things but this was clever and neat. The secret of it was that the fish when disturbed took refuge in the darkness of the tunnel. When the man holding the net entered the tunnel the fish again went upstream, but on reaching sunlight again at the other end they turned back into the outstretched net. Jonathan explained to me that some of them get away by going down by the sides of the tunnel. This was a really clever trick. **Although I have mentioned explosives and chemicals I have never used them on any poaching job in my life**. I class these stupid methods as murder not poaching.

One day I was out with my gun, a Winchester rifle, and met a farmer in a by-lane. While I was talking to him he told me that he wanted some rabbits catching up because he was just setting up a big poultry farm. He was one of the leading men on poultry farming in the Midlands and had taken over this new farm. I knew that there were a lot of rabbits on the farm and it was also next to a huge area of wild hilly land now owned by the National Trust. On top of this he also held the grazing and shooting rights on all this huge piece of land. On all National Trust signs it says, no snaring, no trapping, no shooting is allowed, but it is. I asked him to keep all people off for two weeks, shooters and others. He agreed to this course and in the meantime I got the snaring tackle ready.

TEAMING UP WITH A CASUAL

Unfortunately Jonathan was ill at the time so I took along another man to help me. I was at work all day setting snares and quite a few rabbits were caught at dusk. The next morning we had a good haul to take home. This farmer came to us when he saw us on the fields and was very well pleased at our efforts. Later he gave me a permission note to allow me to go on his land night or day and to use any method I liked, including the nets. I had a lot of rabbits off that place and that permission note covered me for a lot of poaching jobs carried out on other places. In a long time of poaching, trapping, snaring or shooting this farmer was the only one who gave me full freedom to do as I wished. He never asked for as much as one rabbit.

The man I had taken with me must have been talking 'out of school' and the place was being upset by prowlers. I was having rabbits taken out of the snares and I found out that this man was one of those responsible. This comes of doing someone a good turn but still one has to pay to learn what people really are. A few weeks later I took steps to let slip the fact that I had set some snares on a certain woodside. This was on one Saturday night and I lay inside the wood waiting. Two of them came along but there were no snares set. I do not wish to say what happened but believe me they did not trouble me again.

This poultry farmer was badly troubled by foxes in his early stages, from the great stretch of wild lane. He also showed me fox earths on other people's land. I had a Winchester rifle so I thinned out a few foxes. Those fox earths were visited on various daybreaks in the spring months when they had cubs to feed. For this kind of thing one has to have the patience to wait and must understand the wind positions. I did the same thing on a few other places. If one uses a shot gun for this sort of work he would have to be within fifty yards of the earths whereas a good rifle shot can keep over a hundred yards away. The best time to shoot is when the fox stops in front of the earth. One farmer in this area asked me to catch up some of his rabbits. I took on the job but I was stopped inside two weeks. He could not rest and was always around to see what I was doing.

Some farmers hate to see anyone else get anything from the land. This did not make much difference to me, I could use the nets at night-time.

Poaching Incidents
and Personalities

5

Figure 5.1 Weasels, great rivals of the rabbit poacher; there also existed great rivalries between we human poachers.

POACHING INCIDENTS AND PERSONALITIES

About this time two of my young nephews who had been out after birds' eggs told me about a place they had seen and it was alive with rabbits and hares. I had poached on this place in previous years and it had been given a long rest, in fact it was the same place where one of my friends was arrested when he got away with "Costs of Court". I had a good look round and about October I took another man with me with the nets. We had some good catches when we started on the place and then a mistake was made. My so called friend was taking other people to the area at times when I could not go. Three of them got caught and they got a heavy fine and loss of nets.

A DRY SEASON

I was given some information about poachers trying to work an area in the West of our county and they were getting very poor results. It was a very dry season and the ground was baked hard with the result that nets would not stand to their work. Another thing that may have been happening was that heavy boots could sound like drums on the hard ground and this is fatal to good poaching. Jonathan and I had a good look round the whole area and decided that we would have a go. While we were actually at work on the job we were wearing rubber running shoes as footwear and we were using specially made steel pegs. These pegs were dipped in green enamel so that they would not chink or rattle while being used. They are dangerous things if one happens to stumble in the dark, but they do marvellous work.

Other poachers could not make out what we were doing to catch so much game and this led to incidents of jealousy. There was indeed a great deal of jealousy and rivalry among the poachers. One must bear in mind that these were the years of hardships due to lack of work. It may seem curious but I have known poachers all over the country and have never once come across any single one who used steel pegs. To give an idea of what this area of country was like I took over two thousand

83

rabbits off it in the early years of the war working alone. Jonathan was in the army. The biggest problem was transport due to petrol rationing.

CHALLENGES

A well known land owner some miles out of Eccleshall used to let his shooting and trapping at high prices. He knew that I had been in court for poaching and he said that no poachers would take his, because the best area was bounded by a river and marshes. He thought the only way on was through his farmyard where the dogs would create a barking racket. The farm house was facing some big sandy warrens, half a mile long close to the river. He was wrong, there was one crossing place in that valley right behind the warrens. It had been shown to my by my old trapper friends. These warrens were flat and old John's teaching was to pay off. We bont lined those warrens time after time. Off these warrens two of us once broke all known records for two men in those years.

The man who I mentioned earlier from the Southern part of the country rented the trapping rights on two adjacent estates. I was told in the early summer about this. He had made the deal early in order to prevent anyone else trying for it.

Later in the year when rabbits and so on were saleable we visited both these places. I had not forgotten him for what he had said to me about poachers having no chance where he came from. More than a thousand rabbits were cleared off before he started his trapping. I think using steel traps was about all he knew. One Saturday night I was in a certain hotel alone with my wife and friends. Two of these trappers were there too, and the drink began to open up the conversation. One remark was, "You'll have to watch your rabbits or the poachers will be at them." "Oh, no they will not take mine. I'll stop them poachers," came the answer.

We had taken more than what we termed our share and there was really no need for us to keep on visiting this place to run into trouble. As our party of friends were leaving the hotel I turned to both men and said "I already know to over one thousand that you will not catch. I warned you in Meece that one day you would learn a lesson. You should not challenge people's abilities." Both these men knew that I had been in court for poaching and they were in a way trying to tell others in the room. They did not know that my old trapper friends used to work on these places, and I knew every wood and spinney on the area. This trapper could not have made a lot of profit out of his early deal and later he took up a job as underkeeper.

84

Figure 5.2   The trapper of old.

POACHING WITH MINERS

During these times two mining men from Nottingham and Yorkshire asked me to show them something of the night game just for an experience. They had their own motor and we agreed to take them out just once. Jonathan and myself took them out beyond the Shropshire border. We caught about seventy rabbits and one hare. Half the night was spent in explaining to them the various moves of the game. This was in the Shifnal area and when daylight came they were surprised when they saw what a lovely countryside the Shropshire border and North Staffordshire can show. One of them said he had been told that I knew my way about and would I take them on a long daytime run.

The following weekend I took them out for the day to some lovely places and to visit various people who I knew. That motor was like a greengrocer's shop and our last call was at Meece to visit an old friend of mine who was seventy-five years old. It was at his cottage that my old trapper friends used to meet. The old gentleman related some of our escapades to them in the village inn. They were really interested in his stories. In the inn listening to all this was our friend from the South. He started passing sarcastic remarks about poachers and thieves, but his remarks only caused further laughter in the room. I think the two trips were something that these two would always remember. In later years one held a good position in a Sheffield steel works, and the other one got to be a colliery Manager in India.

COCKY AND THE LAW

There was one old hand at the poaching game who was a well known character in himself. He was known to us as 'Cocky' on account of the curious hats he used to wear. He had been caught and when the prosecution came up we decided to go and listen to the case. This was only one of his many appearances in court and there is always something to learn. His case was called out and he stood in front of the 'Bench'. W.P. you are hereby charged with poaching on such an estate, on a certain date and so on. The Magistrate asked the Court Clerk for the evidence and Cocky's net was shown to the 'Bench'. One of the Magistrates said, "Is that a poachers net. It looks more like a clothes line to me." The answer came very sharp, "You would not think so if you had your big red nose fast in it." "Get that man out of here at once", said the magistrate. The case was over and I would think it was the shortest case on record. His fine was stated later. This old poacher lived to see his ninetieth birthday.

Figure 5.3　We were poaching in a small spinney.

Figure 5.4　Ferret and rabbit.

87

A BRUSH WITH A POLICEMAN

One night three of us were out and we had a fair number of rabbits. On our way home we decided to call at a place known as the "Pyebirches". My two friends were to run the nets on a certain small spinney which stood alone. I was to wait in the lane with the motor. A motor cycle stopped at the lane junction and a policeman began walking towards me. I made a sudden start up and off I went. I made a circular tour out towards Woodseaves. After a short while I went back and was creeping along the lane slowly. I picked up one man and the rabbits he had. Higher up the lane a voice was heard "Is that you."

"Yes", came the answer and the next thing that happened was, "Catch these", and our poacher friend was throwing rabbits to the policeman. We called to him to run for it and we managed to pick him up as the policeman called "Stop", but we were away. The man I picked up first had a few convictions for poaching. When we checked up apart from the rabbits which were lost our losses were a pair of driving gloves, two hats, and a large flask. I wondered what was in that man's mind that morning, but anyhow he had some ready caught dinners.

PROBLEMS WITH OWLS

One amusing incident I remember happened one night in the Wootton district beyond Alton Towers. Three of us were out and the nets were set in the Wootton Hall grounds near the lake. It was a half moon night and while going down the nets an owl struck at a rabbit at the same time as one of the men reached for it. That owl gave a horrible screech and then flew at the man. It took him some time to get over the sudden shock. The same thing happened on another night. Two of us sat under a large tree and suddenly an owl made a dive at us. This happened a few times until we realised that were sitting under the nest. In this countryside a certain gentleman lived at a place known to us as "Captain Bradley's" glasshouse. It had some notable history back to Cromwell's days. On moonlight nights he would be wandering about and if he heard any rabbits squeal in the nets he would start yelling at the top of his voice, and banging away with a twelve bore gun. Strange to say this was not the only place where we met moonstruck people. I could not possibly record here the names that man called us.

THE WAR YEARS

After this for nearly four years during the war I worked alone for much of the time. Work of course picked up and the poaching was done at weekends. Now a slight dig at that author who said no man could work long nets alone. I did very well during these years and a good many

Figure 5.5   Owls could sometimes be a problem.

people had a dinner when food was on rations. I had some very narrow escapes during this time, what with our own police and Special police, military people, and fire watchers on the big woods. Not many people realised that the countryside had fire watchers. I met a few of them while I was out.

During the war years I had a friend who owned a big Rudge motor cycle which was very useful as long as we could get petrol. He asked me to show him how the night work was carried out. He was in no way a poacher but he said he would like to see the actual job carried out. I took him out with me and it created quite a laugh for me to see a real novice on his first night out. On one hedge side I was going down the nets killing the rabbits and I saw my friend gently put his foot on a squealing rabbit and I heard him say, "Keep still till my pal comes". That man did for me a good many helpful journeys with his motor cycle during the years that I poached alone. Very often I would go out by pedal cycle and he would meet me in the morning to bring the catch home for me. That motor cycle has brought as many as seventy rabbits home which is not bad for one man's catch.

One night I was out on a place known to us as "Hatton Pastures" and was working alone. I had actually got my net set when four men came down the woodside on the wrong end of the wind. As we met I said, "No further. I have a net down and keep your feet out of it." They began to threaten me and while this noise was going on there came twenty-two rabbits into the net. I flashed my light to make them believe that I was not alone. I said if they interfered with me someone was going to get hurt. I very well knew that my chances were poor if they intended trouble but the bluff worked. They were trying to poach as well as myself. It was as I said when I left them, "You novices are a damn nuisance to respectable poachers. You have a lot to learn yet. You do not even know which way the wind blows."

A New Team Mate

It was during the war years that I teamed up with another man who stayed with me for a good many years. Off the area where I mentioned that I had a good run while working alone we did very well together. He was a good, quick, reliable man with the nets. During the years we were together we had some hectic times. When we could get petrol I took him to lots of places he had not been to before although he had used nets before we got together. He was game enough to go on any estate that I knew. I tried to teach him to know the wind by the stars when they were showing. I also tried to teach him the use of Ordnance Survey maps. This part of the game was left to myself. During our early time together we made one nasty mistake. We were doing very well off a certain area and one night we were stupid enough to take a relative of mine out with us. Within a few days I think everyone who tried a spot of poaching knew where we were working. He was never allowed to be with us again. It is not only a matter of jealousy like some people think. The facts are this. If a place has a thousand rabbits and someone has been at them one night and someone else goes on the next night it is almost sure to finish up with a very poor catch. Rabbits will not run night after night if they have been upset. Plenty of rabbits escape the nets in various ways. One of the secrets of success in night poaching is to give any area a rest between visits.

I took my friend out one weekend to the Bagot's Park area at Abbotts Bromley. When we reached the woods where the motor was to be left we were challenged by soldiers. We were actually putting the car on one of their guard posts. Unknown to us because I had not visited the area for some time the place was being used by the army and Air Force people. An officer who came out to us and demanded to know what we were doing gave us a good telling off. Even if he was an officer, he was no gentleman the way he cursed us. "Poachers, and a damned war on. You have a damned cheek to go poaching when the whole country is under arms. I don't know what the hell you would do in peace time. You will end up getting shot." That ruined that night and, of course, the area was useless to us until well after the war.

AN UNFRIENDLY KEEPER

There was one big estate in the South of our county which held a great deal of all kinds of game from deer to pheasants. I got to know from country people that the deer had been moved by Government orders. There was a huge area of rough fenny land where the deer had been. Two great slices of this land had been ploughed up by Italian war prisoners, and turned to grassland. Each section was over one mile long. I walked across that estate to get the proper wind bearings on these new areas, although I already knew the woodlands. Here is a bit of advice to novice poachers. Always do your daylight trespassing alone. It causes less suspicion although a good keeper is always suspicious of strangers. I think all the rabbits and hares in that huge deer park used to make for the fresh grasslands. There were no hedges on this area and it was ideal for netters. There were a lot of hares and these were sometimes a nuisance to us on account of the noise they made as they hit the nets.

The head keeper on this estate was a very dangerous man. In one instance, we had the nets set not far from his cottage and his dogs either winded us or heard something. The dogs began to bark and create a racket and the keeper was out quick. I ran for the field gate in case the hares struck. My intention was to prevent anything from squealing but I was too late. The hares were squealing and I could just see the keeper and one of his dogs coming towards the gate. I was waiting for him with my usual powerful flashlight. My friend was busy taking up the nets. Instead of that keeper coming right up to the gate he stopped about 25 to 30 yards away and let go with both barrels of his gun. I was behind the stone gatepost keeping very still. My friend had also flattened out under cover. "Who's there?", he called, but there was no answer, all was very quiet. I do not fancy being the target for a shot gun. It may seem strange to some people but that keeper was liable to a heavy penalty for that trick. Our position was like this, we were both breaking the law. That keeper did not come any closer, why I do not know. Anyhow we got away all clear with some rabbits and two hares. That keeper was one of the meanest men on that countryside. Not once did I hear a good word about him. Everybody hated him.

I knew one tenant farmer who actually went into this keeper's cottage in a temper and struck him for some reason, but I do know that this farmer had no scruples about snatching a pheasant or two. This keeper and two other men once came at two of us for picking mushrooms. When we showed fight, to our disgust he was armed with a loaded cosh. The quarrel carried on to the road and someone sent for the police to stop the trouble. That keeper went off in a hurry on his motor cycle and the other two also ran away. When the police arrived they asked where he was and what had happened. They took us along and one can imagine that

91

Figure 5.6 Deer were to be found on the estate.

keeper's surprise when the police and us entered his yard. The interval had given him time to get rid of that cosh. I described it to the police and he was warned that if he was caught with a cosh he would almost certainly get two years in prison. The police said this was not the first time he had threatened people.

I knew one old gentleman seventy years old, who had a basket of blackberries taken off him by this keeper who kicked them in the air. I told this gentleman that we had been night poaching on this estate and he got me permission to park a motor on a certain farm any time I wished. I have parked a motor at all hours of the night off that farm drive and no questions were ever asked. I am glad to say that man had more than the value of those blackberries in dinners. It was a good job for that keeper that guns were out of the question due to the war. Even my favourite Winchester had been taken over by the police or I might have snatched a pheasant or two. There was everything on this big estate from wild ducks to a nice trout lake. The old time poachers would have hit him with everything they could for carrying that cosh. The land that I mentioned, being reclaimed for grass was a little gold mine to us. Even after the war ended and my old friend Jonathan came home from Italy we three had almost five hundred rabbits in a few nights. One of Jonathan's cryptic remarks was this. We had set three eighty yard nets in a valley on the edge of the deer park. The moon suddenly broke through the clouds and the nets could be seen waving in the moonlight. As we waited for cloud cover he said, "It looks well. If those keepers come they cannot accuse me of not trying."

GUNS AND RABBITS

There was one place that was all big woods and one had to know the rides of the woods in order to get at the best places. During the war a huge dump was put in this area. There were gun turrets and machine guns at various spots. For some reason no one was allowed to catch up any rabbits. Of course this is typical of the faceless wonders. It was strange to me because we had hundreds of rabbits from here even when the war was on.

POACHING IN STYLE

On one occasion a man who owned a factory wanted to go out with us to see what a night's poaching was really like. I guessed that his real idea was to get to know something for his shooting friends. My friend persuaded me to take him just once. We went out in his car, a big powerful limousine. We had decided to go to an estate in the south of the county and when we got there it was awkward to find a place to park this

93

big car, so we took it just inside one of the estate drives. A piece of notepaper was fastened on the car to say that it was out of order. The notice read, "Please do not touch. Out of order". The car owner did not understand, why the notice? The next morning when we went for the car the move was successful. No-one had even been near it. When he was told later what had been done, that was the end of night poaching for ·him. During the night we were moving from one wood to another and as I approached the particular spot to get on the woodside a young bull lay right in my path. I was poking him gently with a stick trying to get him to move quietly. I did not want any noise. Suddenly things happened, our novice friend had crept up to see what was going on, and he let go with a piece of stone he had picked up. I think all the beasts in that field panicked when that bull roared. I was furious at this stupid action and he said, quite in ignorance, "I thought you were trying to move him", "But how do you expect us to catch anything with that row going on. You have spoiled the whole wood." This meant us moving to the next wood. He was a man who would do a good deed for anyone as I will describe later.

PRISONERS OF WAR

Towards the latter end of the war, the war prisoners in certain parts were allowed more freedom. Two of my poacher friends asked me to take them out on a daylight trip to an estate in Shropshire. It was a place they had never been to and nor had I for some years. During the afternoon we were taking a good look round this place. I was away from my two friends and when I went to a big fir wood I saw two German war prisoners trying to set a snare or two in the hedge bottom. When they saw me they explained in their broken English they were only having a walk round. I told them it was nothing to do with me, but the snares they had set were absolutely wrong. Single strands of wire hanging from the fence above was useless. There were a few snares in the car so I got them and proceeded to show them the proper way. I pointed out the marks on the runs and how to put benders in a hedge bottom. I explained to them the correct height to set them. They were all smiles as my friends came looking for me and they had quite a laugh as they handed cigarettes out to the Germans. I took the two Germans to a fresh spot on account of the trampling that had been done, and I left the snares set on good runs. I suppose they wanted a change for dinner, and I knew that we would not be able to poach on the place until well after the war. This estate was visited a few times after the war.

JONATHAN RETURNS

When Jonathan came home out of the Army the three of us worked together. It may be a wrong thing to say but I have known a lot of men who have tried a bit of poaching, and I knew their capabilities. I would have been willing to back we three against anyone in the Midlands.

One good turn which the factory owner did for us was just after the war had ended. Petrol was still rationed then, and in order to get out we pooled together and were using a van. We had the intention of going on an estate near Market Drayton and we had only half a mile to go when suddenly things went wrong. A car was parked under the overhanging trees on the road side with no lights on and we sailed right into the back of that motor. A couple were in that car. We were out of that van in a flash. Poaching jackets, nets, and other tackle were flung into the woodside and my two friends also took to cover. The man who was in the car did not even see my friends nor the poaching nets disappear. There were no personal injuries but both motors were damaged and the police were sent for. The lady in the motor had disappeared when the police arrived and I asked our driver what he intended to do. We did not relish the idea of bringing ladies into the case, because we had got enough to contend with. We kept strictly quiet about the lady. I told the car driver that we had seen the lady and it was up to him to keep quiet about her if he wished to. After all particulars had been taken our van was pushed into a ride of the woods to clear the road. I stayed with the van all night and also to take care of three valuable nets. The police got our driver a lift towards home, but my other two frends were faced with a twelve mile walk. When everyone else had cleared off I went to them in the wood to talk about the best way home. There was nothing else for it, if they stayed with me we might all get into trouble. Their nets and other tackle were all put together and I was to stay the night with them. When they had gone I was busy hiding the nets by the roadside when suddenly the police constable appeared again, and I had not heard him coming. He was riding a cycle with a very low light. I lay flat where I was on top of the nets which I had not yet covered over. He examined the van again and had a look round. I was wondering what was in his mind. I knew that if he spotted me and the nets not yet covered over, then the game was out for sure. Eventually he walked away and I covered the nets over with ferns and grass. I decided to have a sleep in the van because I had a long wait in front of me. I was asleep in the van when the police constable came again and wakened me up. Now then, I thought, what the devil is upsetting him. I knew that I had to be very careful. One slip and we should all be in trouble. He said, "You were not here when I came up a while ago." My answer to him was, "Oh, I must have been in the wood for my own reasons." He told me, "I have seen two men

95

making towards Newcastle and they look to me like poachers". "Poachers, what do you mean? That is something new to me", I said. He replied, "There is a lot of game about these parts and some men will try anything you know." I asked him what these poachers did in the dark. He did not know much about the actual methods used, but he knew the penalties all right. What a nice calm conversation this was and only a few yards away were three valuable nets in the ditch. I was thankful that he had not got a dog with him. My mind went back to my days with old John and that unfortunate police man who lost his legs. This happening was in the same countryside. In regard to the policeman's statement of a "lot of game in these parts" Red Hills was one of the loveliest parts of Staffordshire and among the best cared for.

Word was got through to my home and steps were taken to get me home. Get yourself into trouble and one will soon find out what people are really like. My wife went to two neighbours who had cars. I had supplied them with game all through the years of food rationing. They just did not wish to know. They could not do anything. "No petrol" and other excuses, but this did not deter them from informing all in our local hotel that I was in serious trouble and other silly comments. This hotel was where a lot of our catch was sold. Our friend the factory owner, as soon as he knew got his car out to get me home. He was told the district I' was in, and all our nets and tackle were got safely home.

There were some aspects about this affair that I never really understood. When the case came before the court our van driver was fined for careless driving, and a discoloured window screen. I myself was not even called as a witness; nor was any mention made of the other motor having no lights on. He was not even asked what he was doing to be parked there. I have often thought that man was someone well known and was "covered" as much as possible. It was a case of "who knows who". Even in regard to us no questions were asked on the use of petrol which was still under rationing. We were not even questioned as to why we were there at night time.

If anyone had done something wrong to give our game away it could have meant nets confiscated, a heavy fine under the poaching laws, wrong use of petrol, plus the driving fines. That was one of those nights when "Lady Luck" had deserted us, but not altogether. My two friends had tired feet and we were several pounds out of pocket but it is all part of this game.

Return to Normal Conditions

6

Figure 6.1   Group of British birds: the narrow escapes from the law of my later years were a far cry from the days when illegal exploits merely consisted of bird's nesting.

RETURN TO NORMAL CONDITIONS

A NARROW ESCAPE

When Jonathan came home from Italy a soldier friend of his got him permission to go on his father's farm, about five miles out from Chartley. Three of us were out and we had gone by car to the estate of the nasty keeper I have mentioned. Everything was quiet enough during the night and we had ninety or more rabbits and two hares. If my memory is to be trusted I think it was Christmas Eve. Everything was ready for home and we were waiting for the car, but no car arrived at the appointed time.

Something had gone wrong so we decided to ditch the game, and the nets. We began to walk the road in order to keep ourselves warm and hoping to meet the car. We had covered about two miles when a car was seen coming towards us. "Look out", I called, "Here comes the motor". I waved my flashlight to let him know that we were on the road. The car flashed past us and we saw that it was a police car. "Look out, boys, it's the police. Be careful and leave things to Jonathan." The car had stopped and was reversing back to us. One of the policemen called out, "What are you lot doing at this time of the morning?" Jonathan answered him very calmly, "Oh, it's alright, officer, we have been after some rabbits, but our car hasn't turned up." At this they got out of the car and said they would search us.

The first thing was that I had an American army flashlight. The policeman said, "Where have you had this from? It's American army stuff." I replied, "Yes, and so is the one you are using." Both flashlights were of similar type. I laughed because I knew that was that in regard to flashlights. These lights held five batteries and had a top beam up to a hundred yards.

We were searched and only Jonathan had any identification, some army papers and his permission note. "How many rabbits do you reckon you have caught?" asked the policeman. Jonathan told him. "Ninety odd, sir." "Who do you think you are kidding?" came the answer. They told us to wait while they talked things over and then they said, "You two get in that car, and we will have a look at these rabbits." Jonathan and I got in the car and he whispered to me, "Creswellshawe Hall farm?" "I don't even know where the blazes it is," I replied. "I do, be careful." We picked up the rabbits, hares, nets, and pegs and the back of that police car was loaded. "Now then," said the police sergeant, "We will find out the truth, but we must take you to see this farmer first."

It was a good thing that I had a good knowledge of that countryside. "Move on. Straight on for a few miles until you reach the river Blythe. First turning to the left and second farm up the lane." Jonathan stared at me and gave me a dig in the ribs. When we reached the farm the police banged on the door until the farmer answered it.

When he opened the door the police sergeant began asking a lot of questions. He said, "My son fixed Jonathan with permission to catch some of our rabbits. There is a lot in those woods and they don't tell me when they are coming. They come when they think it is fit for them, and it's quite alright as far as I am concerned." After an argument the police sergeant agreed to take us back to where we had been picked up in case our car had arrived. "Get in you pair of cheeky blighters." We were taken back to our other friend who had the sense to stay where we had left him and the car was there. The constable asked us for a nice fat rabbit for each of them and we were only too willing having won that little battle of wits and nerves. A few minutes later we were on our way home. This was a very ticklish time and not many poachers can say they have had a ride in a police car along with all the night's catch and still get out of trouble. What we could not understand was why they did not query the fact that it was not possible to carry ninety rabbits and nets for five miles. In fact some of them had been caught close to where we had left them. It was well on to mid-morning by the time we got home.

THE GREEDY FARMER

I knew one farmer who was reputed to be a wealthy man. He was very greedy. He would employ an old hand to trap the rabbits for him at a price per head and then go and steal some of the catch so that he would not have to pay out too much. I knew one of these old trappers personally and he told me about this. This farmer was so greedy that even during the war he was overcharging service men for various farm products. One day after the war I had taken my poaching friends for a day's run in the countryside. We visited a lot of places on the Shropshire border, and eventually called at a certain country hotel for a drink and lunch. This greedy farmer land owner was in the bar room along with other farming people. I was known to a few of these people and soon the inevitable subject of the poachers came up. This greedy farmer stated the fact that he had a nasty Alsation and no one would dare to go near his place. I had already been given information that the dog was dangerous, and I had also seen the big brute. Jonathan and I were near the bar and Jonathan said, 'Mr. . . . , there is a way to deal with nasty dogs like yours. If ever that dog does anything to anyone I know I will cure him for you with a twelve bore."

Jonathan asked him if he remembered a man who once owned a black retriever a few miles away and what happened to it. This black dog was owned by a man who had no connection with the land, but the dog was always loose at night-time. He had twice attacked night poachers and bitten two of them to my own knowledge. He once came at Jonathan and myself before the war, but we always carried flash lights and these may have saved us. One night someone had gone to this country house and called the dog out of his kennel. He was met with two charges from a shotgun and no one ever knew who had done it. I know this may seem very nasty, but it is the best end of dangerous dogs. Shortly after this hotel meeting the police had this Alsation destroyed for attacking a cyclist on the road.

Believe me, to deal with a nasty dog at night time is a terrifying experience which would break the nerves of some men. As soon as we knew about the Alsatian's end we hit that man's rabbits really hard.

Figure 6.2   Black retriever; one of this breed proved a great danger to night poachers. Many farmers let vicious dogs loose to attack unwary poachers.

101

TWO TRAGEDIES

One never knows what can happen in this poaching game. I know of one man who was killed while out poaching on a place known to us as the "Black Woods". I very well knew that if these statements had been made at the time of happening someone could have been in serious trouble. I personally knew both of these poachers who were out that night. I was on holiday at the time down in the Thames Valley and when I came home word was brought to me about this man and what had happened. He had been attacked by a bull. He was found terribly injured lying beside a small stream. A passing motorist happened to stop on a small bridge and saw him. He died later that day at Stafford. At the inquest a verdict was returned that he had been struck by a non-stop motorist. Someone tried to cover up the fact that this man was poaching.

Only two weeks before he was killed I had sold him two nets and I had also met him when out. If it was true what I was told by various people there could have been several people involved in trouble. This case was no concern of mine and possibly it was better to let 'sleeping dogs lie'.

Another dangerous thing happened one night when we were out. This concerned the ex-army sergeant I have mentioned before. We were crossing a stream with a good catch and the crossing was a single plank. The plank was wet and our friend slipped with the bag of rabbits on one side of the plank and him in the water on the other. He was being choked and it was lucky for him that I had a good knife. As I cut the rope on the bag to release him he went backwards into the stream. As he scrambled out I was trying to find the bag. We recovered the bag but some of the rabbits were lost. It left our friend with a badly bruised neck and he was grateful that I took quick action. To break the tension of the moment I told him in jest, of course, that the losses would be deducted from his share for his carelessness. This kind of thing can happen when crossing deep ditches.

A SERIOUS MISTAKE RESULTING IN ARRESTS

Two of our local poachers were caught in an area known to us as the Tradswell Woods. It was full moon at the time and we had decided to give the poaching a rest because we did not fancy the night. These two men were foolish enough to park their motor in a field near some poultry sheds. This to my mind is simply asking for trouble and it is something that I would have avoided at any time. What happened here is the fact that they had given no thought as to what time the moon would rise. While they were at work a farm hand who was going home late saw the car in the moonlight and he immediately informed the farmer that poultry thieves were on the place. The police were phoned for and the

Figure 6.3 Chillingham Cattle — bulls can be a danger to the poacher.

farmer took steps to padlock the gates. Two policemen arrived by car and they had to wait for the owners of the parked car to show up. When the poachers came up to their car they had some rabbits. I happened to know both these men and they told me that when the farmer knew that they had touched nothing only rabbits which were not even on his land he asked the police to give them a warning to keep off the area. He did not wish to press the case, because the rabbits had come from the nearby estate. This did not please the police sergeant, possibly because he had been called out, and he took the case to court. This was the case I have referred to when they were fined £50.

As soon as I knew about this happening two of us hit that place fairly hard for a short time, on the grounds that no one would be expected to visit the area so quick after the heavy fines. Eventually my friend made a slight mistake. He had left behind a few rabbits which had been tied together for carrying and if they were picked up the evidence was very obvious. Rabbits do not tie themselves together! During the time that we gave this place a little attention we were nearly caught twice. The narrowest escape was on one Saturday night. We had put the motor behind a new house which was being built in a back lane. We had covered the motor with a brown and green camouflage sheet and this saved us from being caught. We were ready to move on to the woods about eight hundred yards away,when two men came off the lane and looked around the new house. One was a country policeman and they almost walked on us. My friend's head was quite close to one man's feet. After a look round they walked away from us and could not possibly have seen anything. Anyhow we decided to stay and we had a really good haul. This was the same night that my friend left a few rabbits behind him on the fields. It was breaking daylight by the time we had got our catch to the road and it was too late to go back. It would have been a bit of a shock if we had been arrested and taken to the same court. After this we kept off that area for a few months.

These two poachers came to see me at home in an effort to get me to take them out. They knew that there were one or two farms where I could leave a motor, but one snag to this is that even among farmers the less they see the better. The less they know the better or some of them would have been wanting a share of the spoils. I liked to poach for myself and not for other people. On the other hand some people never seem to respect a privilege.

END OF A PARTNERSHIP

After a good many years as poaching friends the partnership between the best three men was broken up due to two of them being injured in mining accidents. Although we were friends for a lifetime we could not always work together, but I have never in a long life worked with better poachers since my days with old John. Here is an example of what they were like. We were off work due to some dispute and in one week we were out four times and not once was our catch less than one hundred. The top catch was one hundred and sixty, and this was off the area which the Italians had reclaimed during the war. These two friends of mine were known as well as I was and never once in all those years did they ever refuse to tackle an estate. Like everything else all things come to an end and 'Father Time' waits for no one. Jonathan passed on in 1976, but I often think about the times we had together. The other one was named Edward. I have made this statement before and I do not mind if anyone thinks it is boastful. I would have backed these three against anyone in the Midland counties.

A NEW PARTNER

People may not believe this but during the rationing years if I had been on shift work there would sometimes be a phone call from my friends to say the night was good and the motor would be at the gates. My work friends used to look forward to our rabbits. During the last six years of my poaching escapades I took on another friend. He was good in some respects. I have stated before in this writing that I had a vast knowledge of our countryside and after a few nights out on various places, I took him out to places inside Shropshire where I had never taken anyone before. Not even my old friends. It does not do to show everything even to friends, because there are times when even the best of friends part company as time goes on.

During these last six years of night poaching we had some really good catches for two men. As many as one hundred and fifty rabbits in a few hours. In these Shropshire districts some of the estates had open roads with steel cattle grids at the entrances. On these places we often took the motor in quietly with no lights and loaded up in the estate itself.

In the six years that we worked together our lowest catch was sixty-six and our top catch was a lot over two hundred. We topped over one hundred on fourteen occasions. I have shown this man poaching areas from Derbyshire to Shropshire as well as our own county. There was one lovely estate which was well cared for by keepers and estate workers. It was a very large estate and the game on it was fantastic. This particular estate also had some lovely lakes and at all entrances were notices stating 'Strictly Private'. No one was allowed on the place according to the locals. I knew my way about this estate and it was really a lovely beauty spot. Poacher or not, I love to see nice countryside and this was one of the prettiest places for miles around.

Figure 6.4 One lovely estate provided grand fishing — as well as deer, pheasants, rabbits and ducks.

106

Along with my friend we have sat quite a few times on moonlight nights on the hills overlooking these lakes and talked of what we would like to do. Why were we not born to be keepers instead of poachers on such a lovely place. Wild deer, pheasants, rabbits by the thousand, hares, and more wild ducks than any place in all the Midland counties. All this besides the grand fishing. What is more pleasant than to watch those ducks flighting in the moonlight. It made one long for a gun and freedom to use it. My friend often used to say, "We wish the keepers a good night's sleep". One year in the month of October along with my friend we netted over five hundred rabbits in four visits to this estate and at no time were we on the estate more than a few hours. I do not know what would have been the results if that place had been hit from dusk to dawn, but it takes time to load up. I often told my friend that one mistake such as a car coming in to the Hall late at night or early morning while we were loading up and we would not be able to get away. Anyhow this did not happen although we had some very narrow escapes while we were poaching the district.

One Saturday night we had decided to park the motor quite close to this estate only one field away. We had just got the motor off the road and put it behind a big haystack when two men with lights came off the road. Those men passed within a few yards of the stack and one actually turned towards us. How they missed us with those lights I shall never know. We waited until they were well down that field and then I swung the motor out. Luckily for us they had left the gate wide open and we were away. I said to my friend, "My, that was a close thing. Where the hell did they come from?" We had not heard or seen them as we parked the motor. After we got away we went to another place about six miles away.

We were working one night on a big estate near Shifnal where the timber fellers had been at work. While my friend was running the nets out under the cover of a woodside, he stopped and said he had seen the glow of a cigarette along the woodside. We waited for a while and then I also saw the glow of this cigarette as we thought and we were surmising to each other as to what was happening. I told him if we were in for trouble our destination would be Shifnal police station. While we were waiting to make a move I saw a cow go almost up to where the light had been seen and I told my friend, that was very unusual. Cows and other animals generally stand staring towards a wood or hedge if they know someone is there. I said to him, "Come on, out with the nets and I will go first." Nothing happened and in that field we caught about forty rabbits. I was curious and began looking for the cause of that light. I found that the timber men had been burning their cuttings and as the place was facing the wind, the wind was causing a flickering light under

107

the pile of burnt wood. These are the mild surprises that the poacher meets in the night. It was as I told my friend, "If he did not have a guilty conscience he would not look for such things."

On this particular estate was a very large hay field which was awkward to net properly owing to being in a valley, and it was very rare to get the right wind on it. The wind for this part would have to be North-West to come up the valley, but it was not good for a lot of the other woods. One night this wind was on, although I do not like the North wind. It is a bad wind for poachers. Also on the outskirts of this estate was a narrow lane. A lot of rabbits were crossing this lane also facing towards the north.

The ordinary hazel pegs were almost useless on this lane because the ground on either side was a type of cinder ash and gravel. These pegs would not stand up to their work. I asked my friend if he had ever used steel pegs. He had not so we took steel pegs with us and an extra net, and I warned him to be careful with these pegs because they can be dangerous. That night proved a real topper. The three nets were set in the hay in quick time. Set properly in a few minutes. When those rabbits struck it was like a bedlam. We were both exhausted by the time we had done the killing. This must have been an all time record for two men although these things cannot be proved. We had killed one hundred and forty seven rabbits in one hit. These were loaded up in the estate. These steel pegs were also ideal on the lane I have mentioned and we set this after loading up the first lot bringing the catch to over two hundred. Off this estate and the surrounding areas we topped over two hundred twice. A few miles from here was a long line of low sandy hills and in one season we had fifteen hundred rabbits out of that sand.

FURTHER OUTINGS

There was one case which I remember and I knew both men concerned in this. They must have thought that night poaching was easy for anyone so they decided that they would have a go, although they knew very little about it. They must have been fiddling about and wondering where to leave their motor at midnight, when the police patrol drew up. They had one net between them and they had not even left the car. This happened some miles out of Eccleshall and a few weeks later they got a heavy fine at that court. My own friend persuaded me against my own judgment to take one of these men out to show him how to get that money back. It was Christmas Eve when we took this man out to a big estate near Whitchurch. This estate had its own private church, probably a relic from the old feudal days when estate land owners and the church ruled everybody. The nets were set in a valley and we did not see the lights on in the church until we were on higher ground. The doors

Figure 6.5 A small, private church on a big estate proved a danger one Christmas Eve.

were wide open and we could see the vicar leading his flock in Midnight Service. As I stood looking right down the church aisles my friends asked me if anything was wrong. "Oh, nothing, I was wondering if the vicar would like a couple. I hope he is praying for us sinners." I turned to my friends and said, "Listen boys, someone is praying if you will listen to those nets. Come on get the beating done." There were about fifty rabbits in the nets for the first set. That night paid that man's own fine, but I did not take that man out to that place again. His next trip was out to the Hawkestone Park area and that was his last trip with us.

On an estate near Shifnal the game keepers realised the fact that poachers had been at work. We had the misfortune to get some young bullocks tangled in the nets, and after the rodeo show was over we found that three pegs were missing. Search as we might and I even covered the ground with a flashlight we could not find those tell-tale pegs. The following Sunday morning we took a pleasure trip out to this estate. I left my friend with the motor at the gates of the estate while I took a saunter along the drives. I was taking a steady walk with a newspaper in my hands as though I was reading it, but my eyes were searching the ground over the edges of the paper. Although a week had gone by there may have been a slight chance that those pegs had not been seen. During all the time that we poached on these areas we had never once heard or seen any other night poachers.

My friend signalled to me that I was being watched and as I neared the gates of the estate one of the keepers came up to me. I acted as though I was quite surprised, disturbing me from my reading. At first he tried to be quite sharp with me about trespassing on private land and so on. "No one was allowed to walk about that place." he said. "I'm so sorry, I did not realise I was doing wrong. It is really a nice place you know." "Yes, it may be a nice place but that is not all. We think poachers have been working on the place." I was a very interested listener and so was my friend. I did not understand poaching and I asked him to tell me something about it, and then the truth came out. He told me a shocking story. "Three poacher's pegs had been picked up on the keeper's rounds," he said and he told me the exact place where they had been found.

"Right by the main drive to the Hall. You would not think that anyone had the nerve to use long nets along the drives. I do not know how they have missed being seen by the cars going to the Hall." I sympathised with him in his troubles and hoped that he might catch the culprits. "It is not a nice thing to steal other people's game," I said. When he had gone on his way my friend had a good laugh and said, "How can you be such a liar, and keep your face straight? You will kill me one of these days with some of your cheeky tricks." My mind went back to the times I had checked on that estate in the moonlight, alone. I knew different ways on it and the rides of the woods. This was one of those places from where we had some good catches. It is needless to say that we left this place alone for a few months. We had plenty of other areas where we could go. In later years after our poaching days were over, notice boards were put up at the entrances to this estate, stating "Tresspassers prosecuted. Guard dogs on patrol." These notices were definitely illegal and yet authority does nothing about it. These types of notices can be seen in several areas such as Shifnal, Newport, Hales, Sutton, Cheswardine, and so on. During the last six years of our poaching my last friend had more game than he had ever seen in his life before. My two old friends had recovered from their accidents and were working together again, but it was only on a few occasions that the three of us were able to go out together again.

One night we three were out on a place a few miles from Newport known to us as the 'Grange'. We were going quite well until on one long wood my friends called for me to go to them. They had caught a billy goat in one of the nets. There was a bit of a struggle to get him out and when we released him he promptly declared war on my friends. He butted each one in turn and bowled both of them over. Of course I had to encourage him because it was so laughable.

This is another of those estates with notices up saying, "Guard dogs on patrol." On this estate was a large piece of scrub land in a sandy basin. There were hundreds of rabbits in it, but it had us beaten for once. We did try to overcome this a few times but we would be lucky if we got more than six out of them.

JOKES AND SUPERSTITIONS

What I have written here is mostly to do with my own personal experiences during a lifetime from a boy birdnesting and using ferrets and dogs to night time poaching with a motor on the job. Even when work and conditions of working class life slowly improved I carried on poaching until the job got too much and "Father Time" was calling a halt. Although I was an underground mining official for over thirty years I still went out poaching in the season. There was one small incident that went against me, but it caused a lot of jokes and laughs.

I had been out after a few pheasants and when I was at home I received a message to report for work as soon as possible. There had been an accident. I went to work in a hurry with a twelve hour shift in front of me. My wife was to send on my food. This was a large parcel of sandwiches made up from a cock pheasant. When I had time to eat I got a shock. The colliers had taken my pheasant and left me two paltry thin

Figure 6.6   A goat got caught in one of the snares.

slices of jam. Their comments on the coal face were "Lovely, mate."

There are a good many more incidents that I could recall both exciting and laughable and some that could have been tragic. I was never troubled about what others thought about me, but I have the satisfaction of having provided thousands of dinners all through the years of poverty and then food rationing. A few old people who lived nearby never paid me for a dinner for a good many years. One old gentleman admitted that he used to listen for the sound of the motor in the early hours of the morning. He used to say that when he heard us come home he knew where to get a cheap dinner.

Anyone would hardly believe that superstitions could invade the poaching game. One of the best of them, my own friend, would never use thirteen pegs or carry thirteen rabbits. He would not use a new net on its first night out and neither would Jonathan. They would use them after they had been christened as they called it, usually by me.

Another one, the ex-army sergeant would rub his hands if he ever caught any black rabbits. His version was, "Oh boy, we have caught the vicar, we shall get some of his flock tonight." I knew some Welsh poachers and good men they were, but they would tell you that if anyone catches any game after midnight on Saturday that it would go bad. On the subject of Welshmen it is a bad thing to compare people but I also know Scottish men, and my own opinion is that the Welsh are better poachers. The Scots are too fond of using explosives. I have talked to some of them about these methods which I consider are dirty and not clever poaching and they will tell you that netted salmon will go dark in colour. To me this is sheer make-believe and is just an excuse for some of their murderous methods. Some years ago there was an article in the press that one man had his hand blown off while salmon poaching. He was facing the sun and misjudged the fuse. It was stated that this happened in the Lake District. This is a very dangerous game for people who do not understand explosives.

In Devon and Cornwall some of the native people are very superstitious. I had a very strange experience once in a seaside inn on the Cornish coast. I was on holiday along with my wife and some people from Oxford were talking about shooting. One couple were talking about their country home where rabbits and pheasants came into their garden and they saw me grinning. I was asked if I did any shooting and I told them that I had, but that I preferred nets to catch game. I told them that I had been a poacher all my life and I would have welcomed those pheasants in my garden. I was explaining the various ways to catch them without using a gun, and believe it or not that room was almost empty in a few minutes. One could feel a kind of tension in the room, and every local man had gone out. I had done wrong to mention nets.

113

Figure 6.7 Cornish fishing scene of old. The fisherfolk jealously guarded their nets from use by poachers.

If anyone ever mentions the use of nets for anything except fishing while they are on the coasts of Cornwall they would see the effect it will have. The natives will leave as quick as they can. My own opinion is that they are jealous of their calling and they think if people catch other kinds of game with nets their fish sales would drop.

These fisherfolk are in some ways strange people to understand. Although their work is hard and sometimes dangerous, they are very superstitious. They also do not like outsiders who understand that they too use what may be termed as poaching methods even in the sea, such as sunken nets and small meshed nets.

In another place near Polperro I had a similar experience. I had seen some very fine, good quality thread on the rails by the quay side. I was making a deal for a good amount of this thread to send back home, when the man asked me what I wanted it for. In my ignorance of these people I told him that it would be used to make poachers' nets. He refused to sell me any of it. He said it would bring him bad luck.

Figure 7.   A spot where Trout could be found

Making Profitable
Use
of the Countryside

7

Figure 7.1 Fishing provides excellent sport and the fish caught are an additional bonus to country living to be exploited by countryman and poacher.

MAKING PROFITABLE USE OF THE COUNTRYSIDE *

I will try to explain some of the various things that anyone who likes or thinks about poaching should know. In the first place any man who is timid or nervous, or afraid of hard work and risk should avoid this occupation. Idleness is absolutely no good to any efficient poacher and he should always even during the Spring and Summer months spend what time he can travelling and studying the countryside. No man born can learn it all. Game moves about to various places and fields change in character each year. My own experience is to have a good knowledge of several areas so that in case of anything going wrong a move can be made. Hit when and where you are least expected and do not visit the same place too often.

As regards nerves learn to control yourself and if things go wrong do not panic. Make sure what is happening because to panic in the night can be dangerous. Here is an example of the rubbish people will read in books about country life. The writer said that the poacher should be a good runner when trouble comes along. I should like to see this writer run with a heavy net and a bag of game. I wonder if this writer thinks that poachers are going to run out as much as two hundred and fifty yards of nets to gallop away and leave them. Keep cool is the thing to learn and make sure what is happening.

USING ORDNANCE SURVEY MAPS

I may be wrong in this next statement but I have travelled to a good many parts of this country and I think I am the only poacher in this country who used and worked off "Ordnance Survey" maps. I have known a good many poachers of all calibres but I have never seen or heard of any one of them using these maps. These maps are invaluable and when they are understood are a source of never ending information.

*Because poaching is an illegal occupation much of this section may appear irrelevant. However, gamekeepers and those trapping with a permit should find these hints of value.

The main point about 'Ordnance' maps is that before going out the wind can be judged correctly. Another point about these maps is the fact that if a man has been to a strange part of the country and has seen any game that he would like to get at he has only to set an 'Ordnance' map of that area on a table and set it to the 'North Star'. This will immediately tell him which particular winds will suit the place he has seen. It is not necessary to see the North Star once he knows its position in relation to his own home. The corners of my home are dead on North, South, East and West.

KNOW THE WEATHER

I have sometimes argued with good poachers as to which winds will suit various places and I was not proved wrong. If anyone goes on long walks and starts at the wrong end the results will speak for themselves. The study of the wind alone is a big asset to successful poaching and the best of the poachers sometimes get beaten by this alone. This is only one reason why I used 'Ordnance' maps. By a careful study of 'Ordnance' maps and the layout of the various areas a man would know what to do if the wind changed in the night. And this does sometimes happen. A poacher with anything like any experience does not like the North wind. I have a few times in my life worked places on a North wind but taken all round this wind is best ignored for any kind of poaching. South, East and West are the main points to study along with the intermediate winds. South West, South East, and so on. One of the best winds for killing game all over the Midlands is East. This wind is dry as a rule and all our record hauls were on this wind. I am not referring to those winter winds at the back end of the year.

It often happens that in the early part of the game season in August, September or October the wind will change to North as it is nearing dusk. Nearly always in this case the wind will drop after dark and the grey ground mists will begin to rise on the countryside. This has often caused poachers to be out on bad nights. Most poachers have come up against these conditions of mist. I myself have been miles from home on several occasions before I have noticed them. The first sign of them is near water and when I have seen them I have gone back home. **Game will not run in these mists.**

A howling, very strong wind is not much good to the poacher. I look at it in this way and also from varied experiences. If the wind is a howler the woods are very noisy with old branches snapping off, leaves rustling, and blowing about and any loose fences will be rattling. The noises of a wood will upset the game and it will not move for the obvious reason that wild animals do not like noise. Stand on a woodside where such things as horse chestnuts grow and listen to the falling of the nuts about October

120

Figure 7.2 Winter prospects. The poaching of ground game is as good as hopeless in frost and snow.

and one will understand why the nets are empty. Too strong a wind will often spin on hitting thick woods and this alone will take your scent all over the place. Even when working on open warrens and low hedges a strong wind will bunch up the net.

A steady mild wind is the ideal thing. Also take notice of the temperature because game does not like cold conditions. The poaching of ground game is as good as hopeless in frost and snow. Game cannot eat frozen food and this is the time that they search for the mosses and lichens on the trees on the out of wind side. A simple way to test the temperature is this. At dusk grab a handful of grass and if it feels dry and warm the night will be good. It is better to stay at home than to go out night poaching in frosty weather. Using ferrets in the day time is a different matter. It is in this hard weather that rabbits and hares will strip the bark off the sapling trees. During these conditions of frost, and due to game searching for lichens, traps set in the hedge bottoms will catch some of them, but this is not the poacher's method.

Another type of very bad night is when there is not much wind about especially after rain in warm weather. The ground mists will be seen to rise as the day gets near dusk. First of all near the water courses and gradually it will cover the whole countryside. It is very rare that any game will be caught on these nights. A very bad point about this type of night is the fact that every footmark on the fields can be seen very plain. If any gamekeeper or other interested people happen to be about in the early morning and see those footmarks they can draw their own conclusions. Any one who knows nothing at all about poaching will notice after this type of misty night the thousands of fine spiders' webs in the hedgerows. This is a sure sign of a bad night for the poachers.

I have never heard anyone explain what happens on these misty nights to stop the game from running. Whether I am right or wrong, my own version is this. The mist clings to their faces and they cannot see to run. Also if one feels at the grass it will feel cold and clammy to the touch. Do not get confused over the effect of rain as against mist. On nights which are a bit showery providing the rain is not too heavy it will not stop the poacher from getting a fair catch, but the work is "mauling" and uncomfortable. This means that one has to be prepared to stand up to some hard work.

If the night is warm and there happens to be a light drizzle of rain I have very rarely set the nets more than three times in order to have enough for one night. This mist and light rain have two different effects. The rain for one thing is warmer. This could be a point of controversy for some naturalist to fathom out the difference. I do not for one moment want anyone to think that I appear to know it all. After a good many years of poaching experience the only main conclusion I have ever

Figure 7.3 Use an Ordnance Survey map to know all the bye-lanes.

123

arrived at is the fact of temperatures. Also that rain, being on the warm side, gives game a comfortable bath. A curious thing about rabbits is the fact that light rain does not sodden their fur while they are still alive. I am still of the opinion that mist clings to their faces and prevents them from running.

COLLECT RABBITS REGULARLY

Regarding heavy rain we did a foolish trick one night on an estate in Shropshire. Two of us were out and we had set two eighty yard nets and the rain came on very heavy. There were about fifty rabbits in the nets, which we killed before leaving them. We left the nets set with the dead rabbits still entangled, and took shelter in a keeper's hut which we knew was in the wood behind us. The rain did not cease and after what seemed a long time we decided to take the nets up and go home. We could not afford to be caught on that estate in daylight rain or no rain, and what a time we had to get off. Those rabbits had gone quite stiff and hard and they were very awkward to get out of the nets. It was breaking daylight by the time they were out and we had to make a rush off that estate to our motor. There were also other rabbits to pick up, plus what had been caught last. Never again after that did we leave any dead rabbits in the nets.

USING MAPS

If a man wishes to gain inside knowledge of any estate and that estate is awkward for daylight trespassing get a detailed 'Ordnance Survey' of that particular piece of country. These maps generally cover an area of five or six miles by four. They give a lot more detail than ordinary maps. Every lane, short cut, ride of the woods, stream and crossing place can be found off these maps. Stand at some vantage point as high as possible and set the map to the land marks. It can then be studied. Maps do not tell what is on the various fields so the next move is to go on a moonlight night to find out. The details on these maps will show the crossing places over streams and rough places and this will save a lot of rough walking. Take notice of every field because it is useless to try and use nets on ploughed fields, or long grass and corn. Pasture fields are first to be considered and it will be found that game will make for clean pastures from other quarters. Go through the rides of the woods and find out where they lead to. These rides often save a lot of walking and in a good many cases will bring a crafty poacher right behind his quarry. A man who has the knowledge of how to get right behind his quarry will always be more successful than a man who has to keep to the open fields. I have stood many times on moonlight nights in the shadow of the rides

Figure 7.4 Hares and also rabbits, have long ears, which are not just ornaments.

and watched rabbits and hares running about, while I have waited for the clouds to cover the moon. This could not be done by approaching across the fields. Another point about the use of 'Ordnance' maps is that they show all the bye-lanes. This enables the poachers to leave their catch on the lane sides to be picked up later. It is not sense to carry heavy game across country if it can be left in a safe place. This of course is when a car is being used.

Take care how you walk at night time and do not thump your heels down. Anyone who thumps his heels down can be heard a hundred yards away and this will soon upset the game. Walk steadily and it will save blundering into obstructions such as broken branches. Quietness is a golden rule to a good poacher. The plan of work should be made long before you approach your quarry so that each man knows what to do without any fuss or noise. A careless walker can put his foot down hard on a broken branch and the sudden crack is like a pistol shot. A man who takes care how he does will often save a lot of fouling of nets by broken branches, barbed wire, or other things.

Another thing to be careful about is when entering fields by the gates. The man who opens the gate should hold it steady if anyone else is with him while they pass through. He should then take care to replace the gate catches exactly as he found them. If the gates will not open do not get over at the latch end, use the hinged end, it is stronger as a rule and will allow you to get over with less noise. Some gates have to be held tight as each one gets over. These points may not seem important but they are. Always think to yourself that other people such as farmers and game keepers are not blind. A poacher who neglects these details will either have a poor catch or end up in trouble.

I have tried to explain how to go through or over gates. These little details are important. A point to study very carefully when working on the land at night time is the background behind you. It will be seen in some cases that climbing over gates, or hedges, or passing over high ground will show a man up against the light of the skyline. This is what is known among poachers as 'Shining' yourself to your quarry. A man who sets a net after 'Shining' himself on the skyline will not catch much off that field. This is a far different thing than getting over gates in woodsides or covered by trees. A man will soon learn by 'Shining' himself that wild nature is not blind and he will often get his reward of a poor catch. The same principle also applies in hilly country which should be the places to work on light nights. This is what is known as working the underhill sets; take care to see that it is underhill. Do not go over the top of the skyline or you will work for very little results.

At all times keep down in the valleys and you will find that if two or more men are working together better results will be obtained by one man only on the beating up and the others on the nets. It is very interesting to a novice poacher to stay at the nets on a moonlight night. He will see plenty of rabbits that get away when they see their fellow kind hit the nets. They will turn away and go the opposite way. He will sometimes see them run the full length of the nets and go round the ends.

There is a method of preventing some of this which I will explain later. As I have explained what happens when the poacher 'Shines' himself to moonlight or skyline the lesson is then obvious. **Always make use of the shadows, wood covers, and the contours of the land.**

Although I have explained about gates, do not climb over these or hedges unless you have no other choice. If it is possible always get underneath these places even if you have to belly crawl. Here is an experience of moonlight poaching. My old friends Jonathan and Edward were with me in the Stanton valleys near Ashbourne. These valleys are a series of wooded ravines with no fences or hedges. We had just set three nets under cover of the clouds when the moon broke through very clear. The result was that the rabbits came downhill in such force that the nets were swept into the ravine and all that we got was a few of them. In another instance we were out in the Broughton area on what was known to us as 'Keepers Banks', long banks with woods in the valley and a small stream. On the top was a four hundred yard flat field and the bont line was being used. I was at the nets and believe me I could see a great number of rabbits along the edge of that bank all lined up in the moonlight. I could be seen and the nets too could be seen on the bankside. Out of all that crowd the actual kill was no more than a dozen rabbits, and in those days I was supposed to be the fastest killer on poaching nets. The mistake we made here was that we had set the nets too far in the open away from the cover of the woodsides. We were trusting to the rabbits to come over the bank in a hurry, but it did not work. The 'bont line' was no use in the valley because of bushes. This goes to prove that on moonlight nights these problems need thinking about and the netters have to be quick and crafty.

I would also stress the point of being a bit careful about how one approaches the fields. Rabbits and hares have long ears and these are not ornaments. When these animals feed, being close to the ground every small noise will be picked up quicker than if that noise is in the air. When you are approaching a field with the idea of netting it give yourself a few moments to size up the situation. Do not let yourself think that if you have worked that field previously, say on a West wind, that the situation on a South or South West is just the same. It can be and again it can be wrong. It takes a lot of study to know how the different winds will affect any series of woods. Once again this is where the 'Ordnance' maps will show the difference. I have known poachers who,

127

if they have had a catch off a field due to being in the wind for once will set that same field time after time and never even think where the wind is blowing. This type of poacher rarely gets a good haul. Once a mistake has been made in starting at the wrong end of the wind it can spoil a whole night's work. I have known of areas where if the wind changed from West to slightly North West or from South to South West or vice versa, it would mean a difference of two to three miles at the start of the night's work. If a poacher does not give very careful thought to wind positions he will work for little or nothing. The poacher should give a lot of thought to these things, the wind and methods of approach. The more he keeps behind his quarry the better chance he will have. Do not show yourself on the skyline or on the corners of woods if you can possibly avoid it. Keep to the shadow of the woods.

I have known of poachers working on big woodlands and when they have set the first field they have done quite well. When they have come to set the next field they have wondered what is wrong if the nets are empty, or the catch very poor. This can be due to several things. Either someone has been too close to the next field or the wind is not quite correct. Valleys and big woods will turn the course of the wind. There is also the fact that rabbits do not stay on one field and when they bolt for home they take their fellow kind with them. Another failure of big woods is when the wind is at right angles. If the wind is only moderate on hitting the woods it will spin, thus taking your scent all over the place. To prove how quick the scent of a man can be picked up if he is in the wrong position take notice of cattle and horses. The horse is the quicker of the two and he will pick up your scent four to five hundred yards away. If you are approaching a place and a horse whinnies and stands facing you, it is proof that you are wrong.

The best wind for the big woodlands is when the wind hits the woods at an angle of say 45 degrees or even less. Take care to start at the right end, and you will find that as you set each field the wind is in correct position to keep your scent and any sounds you make off each field as you work forward. This is what is known as working with the wind on the shoulder.

The best type of country for the poacher is that which is varied in character such as a small wood, then a bank or warrens, open fences, a piece of fernland and so on. The benefit of these places lies in the fact that when one spot has been worked you are not close enough to upset the next place. This then tells you that no two places are alike and each one needs a separate study. If the poacher is working in country which has any flattish sandy warrens take care to approach these places in a direct walk with the wind right in your face. Do not try to get at flat warrens by going at an angle across the fields to them. Some men will tell you that

Figure 7.5　A horse can pick up a man's scent four to five hundred yards away.

these places beat the poacher but they do not, if he knows the correct way of approach. Personally I used to prefer a quarter moon to net open warrens and my friends and I have had some good catches like this.

When you have learned your way about a certain section of country, work out how many fields face South and how many face East or West. One must of course know which fields and woods hold the game. It will be found that in most places where poaching is worthwhile, they can be worked in several different directions. This once again is where the 'Ordnance' map does its work. I knew a lot of big estates where I could travel and work from any point which suited the particular wind. This has sometimes meant a difference of a few miles in the place of starting the night's work.

SELECT THE PROFITABLE NIGHTS

If the poacher will take notice, on some nights he will see the stars shining very bright and clear. Every star in the sky seems to be on show. Also there appear to be patches of light in the sky and not a cloud to be seen. I do not like this type of night, the stars seem to chill the air, and very often under these circumstances one can travel the countryside and will not hear a sound. The cattle will lie quite still even as you pass close by. **Under these conditions I have never in my life had a good catch.** When I have been caught out like this I have packed up and made for home. It is better to be at home than to work for no result.

There are occasional nights when there is no moon at all and if the clouds are low these nights can be black. They are sometimes so black that you could not see more than a few yards.

Now comes a point of controversy in which a good many people will say that I am wrong. After a lifetime on the poaching game plus other country pursuits, I will stick to my point. The point of argument is this. No wild animal has better sight than a healthy man. I mean a man who works outdoors and does not suffer from eye strain such as is experienced by industrial workers. If the night is so black that a normal man cannot see to walk then the game cannot see to run either and you will end up with hard stumbling work and get very little for your trouble. These black nights can also happen at times if the moon sets early in the night. I have been out on some of these black nights and I have had to find my way off places by flashlight, and I knew my way about. I knew poachers who have been injured due to blackness. **Black nights therefore are useless.**

For the ideal nights take notice of the moon. **Pick your nights during the first three quarters of the moon.** Choose a night of steady moderate wind with enough clouds to hide the majority of the stars and the glare of the moon. You will find that the moon will give enough light through the clouds to allow you to work fast and in comfort. This is what we poachers called 'working in the grey'. The clouds will keep the air and ground surface warm and even a novice poacher will find a great difference between a night like this and the type of nights I have previously tried to describe. If you understand the countryside and you know the wind positions these nights are a pleasure to live through, and very often they provide a memory for the rest of life. A good many times on these nights I have heard my friends echo my own thoughts and say "Oh boy, it's a grand night and a pleasure to be out." What can be more pleasant than a nights poaching in the Autumn when the whole countryside smells sweet and seems to be alive. After some years in the poaching game you can almost sense what kind of night is before you. I have heard good poachers as well as myself say from instinct. "The night is dead. It has no life in it", or the opposite; "The night feels alive and they are sure to run". Take notice that you will always catch more game when the moon is on the rise than you will when it is on the wane. That is why I wrote to pick your nights on the first three quarters of the moon. The moon has some effects on the movements of all wild animals that are born blind. I know that some people will question or wonder at this but it is one of those things in nature that only experience can find out. I kept notes on these points for a good many years.

What happens is this. As the moon begins to rise from new moon to first quarter rabbits and other animals range further afield, and from first quarter to full moon they travel still further. Contrary to the ideas of some people who write about the countryside, more game can be caught even at full moon if the sky has any clouds, than will ever be caught when the moon is in its last few days or on a black night. Some people will tell you that poachers work on dark nights, but this is wrong. Ground game can be caught during the third quarter of the moon. The game will still be moving far enough out for the netters. It is in the last quarter of the moon that you will get your lowest catches. The only nights that need to be a bit dark are when one is drag netting for partridge. It is quite obvious that it would be a waste of time to go dragnetting across open fields in bright moonlight. A mild night, a steady wind, and a half moon are a poacher's dream.

I was once taken up about this subject of moon affecting ground game by my old friend Jonathan, good poacher that he was. Three of us were out on the 'Hand Leasow Woods' near Chartley, and we had got over one hundred rabbits in quick time, and we decided that was enough for one night. Jonathan said, "That's not bad and that is not on a rising moon don't you forget". I turned to him and pointed out the fact that the moon was seven days past full, in the third quarter. He was not

Figure 7.6 Fish poachers checking the weather — correct conditions are very important for successful poaching.

132

convinced about this subject so I laid him a bet that the following week end we should not get half that number if we worked all night. The following week end neither Edward or myself were out because we did not fancy the night. Jonathan went out with another man to the same woods and believe it or not their catch was two rabbits only.

It took Jonathan a few days to admit this to me, and he admitted they were hopelessly beaten. He had dropped right into the last days of the moon. What happens on the last quarter of the moon is this, with rabbits especially: they are close to their burrows and the woods, and as the poacher approaches they are close enough to see or hear him and, of course, he is too late. They can be heard bolting for safety long before there is time to get a net down.

Further proof of this subject came a few years later. I have stated that the three of us could not always be together. One Sunday morning they came to see me about nets. They told me what a splendid night out they had just had. Three of them had caught one hundred and eleven rabbits. This certainly was not bad but their faces dropped a little when I opened a door and showed them one hundred and fifty which two of us had caught in about three hours. Now this is perfectly true and yet we were working fifty miles apart. In fact in two different counties. We had been to Shropshire for ours.

Anyone who does not believe this subject please take note of the following points. Go into the countryside in the late part of the year when country people and other sportsmen are using ferrets. Note how the rabbits are bolting or, alternatively, how they are not bolting and then check up on the age of the moon. **Rabbits will usually bolt out a lot better when the moon is on the rise.** It is very often in the last quarter of the moon that you will see men having to dig out ferrets and rabbits. Mention these ideas to some people and they would think one is trying to be clever, but it is only too true. Even rats and stoats are far easier to catch when the moon is on the rise.

THE HAUNTED NIGHTS

Although what I have written is from my own experiences as a poacher I still maintain that wild nature will never be fully understood. Here is something that I have experienced a very few times in my life and no one can give the answer.

Occasionally there is the chance that the poacher will be out on what seems to be a perfect night and yet he will get absolutely nothing. I had my first experience of this years ago on an estate near Market Drayton. My old friend John was out with me and the nets were set a few times on various places. The catch was nothing at all. I thought something was seriously wrong and I told John that I thought someone was out-foxing us. He said, "No, that is not the answer my boy. We should have had trouble before this if your idea was right. Now sit down while I explain something to you. This is one of those nights when nature calls a halt and everything on the countryside goes to sleep. The farmyard dog does not bark, geese do not cackle, the night birds are silent, even to the wild ducks and water fowl. The silence of the countryside can be a bit uncanny."

My friend said to me, "This is a real lesson of the countryside for you. One which some knowing people will not believe. It is impossible to pinpoint these nights and it is sheer guess work to say that they happen two or three times in a year, as near as can be told." One must bear in mind that John was a very experienced countryman and he was the only one who ever tried to explain this to me. Since this first night I have come across similar happenings about three times in all the years that I was poaching.

SOME FINAL HINTS

I have explained the useful knowledge of three things in regard to poaching. The use of Ordnance maps, the study of the types of nights which are suitable, and the methods of approach. The next point to notice is your clothes. **Do not wear flappy wellington boots.** Tighten down the leg part because this is the part that causes the flapping. Believe me, the man who wears flappy boots can be heard a hundred yards away at night time. **Do not wear black clothes.** Contrary to the idea that black is all right at night-time it is the worst colour of all for the poacher. Believe it or not black is just as bad as pure white.

Black is very bad for showing up at night time. Black clothes cause a very sharp outline contrast to the colours of the fields, hedgerows, or fern banks, and is easily seen. This point of being seen is in reference to being seen by the game. If wild animals or birds can see a black object moving about the fields they will make it their business to move to safety. If you can, wear brown, grey or khaki mixtures and you will find that they blend better with the fields and woods. I used to wear old clothes of brown and grey tweeds.

This point of colour also applies to good nets. This is another point where I shall be open to criticism, but I am stating from actual experience not what someone else thinks. I have never met any other poachers outside of our own school and heard them discuss the effect of colour on game at night time. To put the matter bluntly, use two nets of equal length, one in shades of green and one in another colour, even to browns and **you will find that the green net will catch the most game.**

During the last war period hemp or linen thread for making nets was very scarce, and we were always on the look out for any thread that could be bought. A friend of mine had managed to buy some black thread from a tent maker and he made a net out of it. As I have explained before regarding colour of clothes, that net was hopeless. He would not believe what I was trying to make him understand, so I had to prove things to him. On a certain pasture field known to us as the "Brooks" near Fradswell a dappled green net was set four yards behind the black one, under the lip of a bank. The black net was untouched because the rabbits could see it quite plainly. They simply jumped over it, but the green net caught twenty four rabbits. These nets were an extreme of colours to prove the point. My nets were dyed in such a way that made them patchy in various shades of green. Even the lines were dyed in patches of green. This has a very good effect.

Years ago when netting thread could be bought in any colour I made two nets and each had probably six or seven different colours all in patches. In order to hear some comment about these, the nets were shown to other poachers on a place where they used to dry their nets. I have always remembered their sarcastic remarks. I got no compliments. One man who had poached with me before, the ex-army man, said, "Don't worry yourselves, boys, we will soon find out if they are any good, and I will be with him." The first time those nets were used was in the Winnington Dales and they killed a lot over one hundred rabbits. Those nets caught hundreds of rabbits and I found them very successful even on places where the game had been well plagued.

I always used colours in my nets until the war came along and one had to be satisfied with anything. After that I dyed my nets to the colours I wanted. The idea of various colours was borne in my mind on that night at Broughton where, as I have stated earlier, the catch was thirteen out of a great crowd of rabbits. The secret of it lay in the fact that when rabbits or hares do face the nets properly and are running alongside, as I explained what happened at Broughton, as soon as the colour of the net changes the rabbits will switch in sideways. The ex-soldier dubbed those nets, 'Old Joey's coats'. He was highly pleased that he was allowed to use them when he wanted. This colour question applies to all nets: drag nets, ride nets, even hare nets set behind gates. One certain writer says that rabbits are colour blind, but not the wild birds. If this man will go ferreting and use brown and green nets he will soon see if they are colour blind or not. As I have said before, these writers have never seen poachers at work or done any themselves.

See that your clothes are in order so that torn pockets do not lose things. I once went to a big farm by the side of the Gratwick woods along with some dealers. They were buying poultry or anything else that was on sale. They asked the farmer if he had rabbits to sell along with the poultry. He showed us two net pegs and said, "How can I have many rabbits for sale when the thieving poachers are using these things?" I hope my face did not look guilty. We had been there two nights earlier. I warned my friends about this. Someone had lost those pegs. This farmer called in professional trappers and that place was no use to us for some time. This is the result of being careless.

Take care of your nets and see that they are of good quality hemp or Irish linen thread; cheap stuff containing jute will snarl and twist up as soon as it gets damp. A good net of eighty yards should not be more than four pounds in weight. On a wet night even this will pull on a man very heavily. One will sometimes hear men boast that they have nets made of silk. Do not take any notice of this, because silk is far too heavy for nets. See that the net has plenty of slack, otherwise part of the net will be stretched like wire netting. A good net stops the game by the shoulders. Take care that the lines of the net are well stretched and perfectly even. If the lines are not even it is liable to upset your work when pegging down the nets.

A net cannot be put down properly if the lines are slack or unven. Pay the net out one loop at a time and keep the lines tight. If the man who is running out the net keeps his eye on the pegger he has no need to be more than a few yards in the front of him. To use a long net by working alone with no help is a far different thing. When working a net alone run the whole of the net out, but take care not to drag the net about too much or it will often foul itself on loose twigs and rubbish. Do not pull the lines too tight and you will find that the net can be back pegged. After some practice at this game one can almost judge how much slack is necessary to peg back. If the poacher happens to be working on woodsides or hedgerows which are not straight it is a simple matter to stick a peg in the ground to keep the net in position. These pegs are then taken out and used as the net is being set up. It is very awkward to describe how to use a net. It is one of those things which work out a lot on common sense and practice. Only continual practice will give a man that touch and feeling in his hands.

Finally, some men are careless as to how they put the net in their pockets and this can lead to getting a net fast when in use.

FALLACIES OF POACHING

I have written before about the author of a book about poaching life. This author says it is impossible for the net poacher to work long nets alone, but he is wrong. I have poached on a good many places alone, sometimes thirty or more miles from home. My best catch using a net by myself was ninety-eight. This means several lifts to get them to the roadside.

In his book, this author tried to describe the use of poachers' nets. He says that poachers pay out the net from a big bag slung around their necks. If any man ever tried to pay out a net from inside a bag he would find himself with one big bundle of trouble. It is quite evident that this writer does not understand poachers' nets or their methods of work. Bags, haversacks, or pockets can be used to carry nets, but bear in mind that nets are folded up and fastened tight in a certain way. They are not put in a bag in loose fashion. To run a net out properly is a job for both hands and very careful hands at that. He also says the pegs or stakes which are used are three feet or more in length and set three yards apart. To anyone, even one who knows nothing at all about poaching, just try to imagine what this really means. A big bag, a one hundred yard yet, and he would need thirty pegs or stakes to be carried regardless of any game. How can a man carry thirty 3 feet stakes and handle a net at the same time. After a lifetime of various methods of poaching I would have loved to see this man in action. I have poached in a lot of places in the Midlands and in other parts of England and Wales but I have never used or even seen any pegs longer than twenty-seven inches and these are classed as long pegs. Also they are used at an average distance of ten yards, not three.

*   *   *

It is not often that poachers use a '**Bonting line**' for the reason that it can only be used on clean and fairly flat fields. These perfect conditions are few and far between, so for all round poaching the 'Bont line' is better left out. The 'Bont' is a strong two hundred yard line on a spinning reel.

*   *   *

In almost every case of countryside authors who write anything about poaching they bring in the inevitable subject of **dogs**. The night poacher does not need a dog for his work, except in the case of gate netting for hares and this is not very profitable. Dogs are, and can be very sporty and a source of good fun, but as to a good night netter, they are certainly not necessary.

I once wrote to a newspaper writer who claimed he had been out poaching. He wrote the usual rubbish about four bold men who were in the village inn until closing time. After closing time they took a walk chatting to each other without a care in the world until they all climbed over a gate into a field and proceeded to run out a hundred yard net on the usual three feet pegs. They then turned out their Lurcher dog who proceeded to sweep all the rabbits off that field while the four poachers

Figure 7.7   A pointer, fine example of a sporting dog, but a night poacher does not need a dog for his work.

and the newsman simply waited for them. How easy! If only my poaching experiences had been that simple. There was no mention of wind, moon, clouds, or the woodside covers. I told this man that **good poachers do not drink before going out**. It is a job of hard work that needs a clear head. Also that when poachers turn out each man has, and is responsible for, his own net.

I asked him how he would train a dog to know how far to go from the nets, and how he would train a dog to know the difference between one hedge and another. One has to bear in mind that various hedges, fields, and woods run at all angles, sizes and shapes. How would he teach a dog not to run a hare or rabbit which would go in the opposite direction to the nets? This would obviously upset the game on the next fields. What use would a dog be to poachers who travel twenty to forty miles from home? I told this writer that all poachers do not live close to their quarry. Some used to travel many miles out. I asked this man to come to my home and we would take him out to see a real night's poaching. He did not even answer me. I have owned and worked with dogs when I was in my teens on all sorts of poaching escapades, both by night and day but in my opinion the man who wants a really good catch does not need to use dogs, although on moonlight nights they can provide good sport for the ferret man who only needs a couple or so for home.

Some years ago when food was scarce and rationed this same newsman wrote an article about poachers going out in Anglesea and North Wales and all they had to do was to shine a light. The rabbits stopped dead still and all that these poachers had to do was to pick them up as fast as they could. I have seen beam lights in use both in Wales and the Isle of Man, and it does not work as he says. The actual effect is to slow down the rabbits as they are picked up in the beam of light. Dogs were trained to take out the rabbits at right angles to the light. The rabbit in the light cannot see the dog coming. The dog that I saw doing this work was a strong black whippet working on the coast line near Port Soderick. In the Isle of Man laws were passed to imprison anyone caught poaching, but three years later these laws had to be cancelled because the rabbits were getting too numerous.

*　　*　　*

One author tells a tale of hare nets being hung over gates with stones placed on top of the gate to hold the net, and some stones to hold the net down at the bottom. Just try to think of the difficulty of trying to balance stones along the top of a gate. This author does not seem to realise that no two gates are alike and in nearly every case the gates are warped and twisted by the weather. He did not mention who was to carry a bag of

139

heavy stones. This is really too crazy. I could set twenty gates against one with this crazy idea. **A gate net only needs two pegs.**

* * *

I once owned a Winchester rifle for some years and I know the methods of approaching pheasants but I do not propose to expose these ideas. There are a lot of ways of catching anything from pheasants to fish and I could make any kind of net, trap, or snare for the job. It was poverty and hard times that caused so much poaching in my younger days. It is a job of skill and hard work and is no job for a nervous man. I met very few really good experts at the game. It amazes me the rubbish about country life and poaching which some writers have the audacity to put in print. Anyone who has done any amount of poaching can pull their statements to pieces. One man writes of poaching his way down the Thames Valley to London and poaching for roach in London parks. Who needs to poach for roach? He then writes of travelling from London to Sandringham in North Norfolk to shoot swans. It must be one hundred miles.

* * *

Another one in a book called *The Poacher* tells of men travelling miles to use ferrets in a wood where they would be hidden from those ever vigilant keepers. How does he expect any one to use purse nets and ferrets in a wood at night time. Also in the morning their Lurcher dog made his way home by a roundabout route to avoid suspicion on his master. This is sheer rubbish!

* * *

One writer says that **buck rabbits** have special areas all to themselves and they fight off other bucks. How does he account for anything like this when two of us once caught one hundred and forty seven off one field, one hundred and twelve, and one hundred and nine off others. He can take it from me there was no scarcity of bucks. One writes of twin brothers named 'Fox'. When one was caught, the other provided an alibi by proving he was somewhere else. Does he think the police are stupid enough not to prove a man's identity? He then writes of a woman named 'Kate' who controlled the poaching in the whole of Gloucestershire. This is one of the biggest game counties in England and a hundred men could not work it. He goes on to say that 'Peers and Bishops' made excellent poachers.

* * *

Roach

Swan

Figure 7.8　One man told of poaching for roach in London parks, and travelling to
North Norfolk to shoot swans.

One article states that rabbits and hares are **colour blind**, but not birds. How anyone works this out or proves it I do not know. After a lifetime of poaching along with my personal friends, and we have caught more game than anyone in Staffordshire, I do know that black, white, red, dark brown, deep blue etc. are definitely out. Also black clothes. This same writer claims that fresh foxes lie in wait when one of their kind is being hunted, and then takes the place of tired foxes. Does he think foxes have human reasoning powers? He writes of foxes killing cats. If a fox tackled a feral cat he would meet up with a real fight. These kinds of writers are just dreamers, and there are many others, who write just such a load of rubbish without having had any practical experience.